WRITING FOR SCREENS

Skills, Tools & Process
for the
Art Of Screenwriting

by Glenn Gers

TABLE OF CONTENTS

ABOUT THE AUTHOR

In his 25-year screenwriting career, **Glenn Gers** worked in a baffling array of genres, including thriller (**FRACTURE**, starring Anthony Hopkins and Ryan Gosling), caper-comedy (**MAD MONEY**, directed by Callie Khouri, starring Diane Keaton, Queen Latifah, Ted Danson and Katie Holmes), family Christmas comedy (**OFF SEASON**), micro-budget horror (**INNER DEMONS**), sitcom (**INSTANT MOM** staff writer) and an audiobook spinoff from the series **HOMELAND**, read by Damien Lewis.

Among his uncredited writing jobs were sci-fi-action and action-comedy rewrites, werewolf thrillers, Biblical and literary adaptations and rom-coms.

He wrote and directed the indie films **LIKE.SHARE.FOLLOW**, (produced by Blumhouse) and **DISFIGURED** (a DIY micro-budget dramedy about an unexpected friendship between two women: one obese, the other anorexic.)

Awards include an **Emmy**, a special award from the **Women's Film Critic's Circle**, multiple festival prizes, **Writer's Guild** and **PRISM** Award nominations and a Fellowship Grant in Screenwriting from the **New York Foundation For The Arts.**

He has lectured or mentored at The Austin Screenwriting Conference, Full Sail University, Cinestory, The David Lynch MFA Program, and the AFI Directing Workshop for Women. His interview on the Film Courage Youtube channel is (for now) their most-viewed video, with over 4.5 million views.

Now retired from screenwriting, he has been teaching on his YouTube channel, **Writing For Screens.** Aside from 50 10-minute lessons -- from which this book is adapted -- the channel features wide-ranging weekly livestream sessions and a video series in which he wrote a full pilot script live online, in 265 hour-long sessions.

BEFORE WE BEGIN

INTRODUCTION

Everything in this book is prefaced with an invisible "in my opinion..."

Writing For Screens collects skills, tools and processes I had to figure out for myself during the twenty-five years I worked writing for movies and television (1994-2019) -- and the eighteen years before that, when I was trying to break in.

When I was stuck or lost, the only thing that got me out of my creative quicksand was reducing the work to a collection of steps to take and things to try, but without a grand system I had to follow.

So that's what this is.

this book does NOT need to be read in order

Each chapter is a stand-alone essay.

I urge you to read all of them, but every artist will need different things at different times.

So I've tried to make the chapter titles self-evident, allowing you to browse the Table Of Contents and seek what you need, when you need it.

The most important thing writing advice can do is send you back to your own work.

My goal is for you to pick this book up very briefly, gather a few bits of advice -- and then put it down and try stuff.

IS THIS BOOK FOR YOU?

This book is intended to help if you:

> don't know how to write a script or a story
>
> don't know how to be a writer
>
> get stuck or lost a lot
>
> have written and don't like the result
>
> wrote something a lot of people don't like (if **some** people don't like what you write: welcome to the world)

I do not know a secret that will make you sell a script or write a hit.

What I can do is try to help you write a better script -- more:

> readable, playable and shootable
>
> narratively and dramatically coherent
>
> emotionally and intellectually effective

I can also try to help you be a better writer:

> more productive
>
> less anxious
>
> more realistic
>
> more aware of possibilities
>
> more capable of working as a professional

I cannot make it easy. I can try to make the difficulty more enjoyable.

MY THEORY OF WRITING RULES

Screenwriting is mostly taught in one of three ways:

The "My Experience" Approach
Someone who's done this thing tells you what they have figured out about how to do it. (This is what I'm doing.)

The advantage: they actually did it.

The problem: maybe the way they did it is just the way **they** did it, and it may not help **you**.

The Academic Approach
We look at great work and analyze why it's great. This is how most of us learn about art in school. It's a very good way to learn the basic elements and history of an art. It shows you possibilities.

But it's not teaching you how to **make** art.

> **the process by which you make something is very different from the experience of consuming it**

Think about riding a rollercoaster versus building a rollercoaster. The builder has to feel and understand the experience of riding -- but also has to think about the design and construction, the working parts, the physics that create that experience, even the "philosophy": what kind of ride do they want it to be?

So as an artist, you have a very specialized educational need -- which the third main system of teaching **is** trying to serve:

The Formula Approach

This says: if you study great art and follow its patterns, your work can be great too. But since you can't just copy the great art: analyze the paradigms, archetypes, structures, messages, methods -- and work within them.

The only drawback: art simply doesn't work that way.

knowing how someone else did it is only part of how you actually create

I can tell you that a great building was built with a hammer, and show you exactly how a great hammer-swinger swung their hammer -- and at the end of all that you will have no idea whether **you** can swing a hammer, and if you can, what kind of thing you can make.

You have to pick up the hammer and try it out, to find the best way for you to use a hammer -- or to find out that hammers are not your thing. Because:

art is a THING YOU DO not a thing you GET THE ANSWER TO

So I think learning to be an artist has to begin with the fact that:

all writing "rules" are only THEORIES

A theory is an attempt to organize the world. It's **one** way of understanding something.

The history of art is full of artists who declared their theory of art to be absolute and final. Most of them had **some** interesting point to make...and **none** of their rules were absolute or final.

Theorists and teachers honestly want to solve the problem of being an artist. People in the art business want reassurance that they're not going to lose their money. Artists want some way to tell if we're doing it right.

But the truth is, there are no rules.

When you create, you are not just working to fill in the blanks -- you are making a thing that does not yet exist. While it's going to partake of the forms of things that already exist, the whole point is: it's something new. You must work, at least in part, from impulse, instinct, emotion and imagination.

Which is, admittedly, scary.

People want art to do different things. Different times and places develop different values for what makes art "good." We even experience the same art differently at different times in our lives.

Most of the current "universal absolute screenwriting rules" were formulated in Hollywood from the 1980s to the early 2000s, by analyzing what was successful at that time -- which is like looking around 240 million years ago and saying: *dinosaurs are the absolute eternal structure of life on earth.*

So, for example, the "rule" that television scripts are broken into 5 acts is simply a "dinosaur" based on how many commercial breaks a show had at the time. An "act" was just a section between commercials, not an insight into the basic structure of stories.

The dangers of creating art according to a formula or rules include:

The Check-Box Problem
You can begin to think giving a label to something or fitting into a pattern assures you that it works. It may not. So much

mediocre work is counting on the formula to deliver, instead of doing the actual work artists have to do.

The Intransitive Magic Problem
The fact that something was great in some other script does not mean that if you put it in your script, then your script will be great.

The Inevitability Problem
Breaking down a finished artwork creates a false impression that it was somehow inevitable, or that you know how it was written. It wasn't and you don't.

That "illusion of inevitability" is one of the most damaging things theory does to artists, because it denies the essential experience of making art:

making art is making choices

**you work it out as you go along,
every single time**

You never really know how it's going to work. You have to make your choice and hope people feel it was inevitable.

(One way to get a sense of how chaotic the creative process is: explore "behind the scenes" and "making of" materials. What you'll find, over and over, is: they couldn't stick to the plan. People and circumstances brought unexpected demands, restrictions, contributions. Things changed.)

Alas, the fact that rules are not absolute or universal **does not** mean they are worthless.

rules (theories) are also valuable

Screenwriting is a difficult, demanding profession which requires specific, obscure skills and knowledge. Rules are often based in very real observations.

And if you want to follow a rule -- go for it! It can make a good script.

But there is no rule to make **every** script.

rules are tools
try them out
bend them, break them, mix-and-match
take what you like, use what you need

**have as many rules & theories
in your toolbox as you can carry**

know how they work

**and then use them only when
they help get this particular job done**

WHY YOU SHOULD NOT WRITE SCRIPTS

Before we get into how you write scripts, I'd like to take a moment to try putting you off the idea altogether.

Scripts Are Incomplete
You're writing a set of instructions for a movie. No matter how you suggest or describe all of the other arts that complete the process -- they're not your job. There are satisfactions and magic in a good script, but it's not a movie.

Scripts Are A Difficult And Limited Art Form
You can't describe much. You can't explore the inner life of characters. Ideas must take the form of dialogue, but you can't have much dialogue.

Add to this the formal and content restrictions set by The Industry, and writing for screens ends up unique among art forms in its lack of creative space.

Scripts Get Messed-With
Seriously. To an extent you cannot truly imagine until it happens.

A screenwriter has no rights to, or control over, a script once it has been sold. The company that buys it will often hire other people to rewrite every word. Many people -- almost none of whom are writers -- will make more changes, based in their own needs, visions or personal agendas. The original writer's opinion will not be sought during this process.

Scripts Are Not Experienced By An Audience
Almost everyone who reads scripts is in The Industry. They read to see if the script can advance their own work, testing it against a set of priorities instead of being open to what it has to offer.

It is great to please these readers -- but it's not the same as reaching an audience.

Scripts Are An Art Controlled By A Business

Every art form has its own complicating layer of patrons, distributors, promoters and facilitators -- but screenwriters are employees. The work can be creative, rewarding and exciting, but it's also often a twisted, ugly corner of art making, and not everyone can handle it.

Most Scripts Won't Get Made

That's just a fact. Even great ones. For a lot of reasons, all of which are beyond your control.

Too Many People Are Writing Scripts

Screen stories stir us so intensely that our creative souls can't help but feel: *I've got to **do** this.* It's a glamorous art, appearing (falsely) to put writers into a universe of celebrities, luxury and fame. And scripts look pretty easy to write: quick-moving and conversational, a lot white space on the page.

This has created a deluge of scripts. Even if yours is good, it's very hard to get anyone's attention.

So then...why would anyone want to write for screens?

It Makes You Better At Storytelling

The essential skills and discipline of writing scripts can serve you well in any other narrative art.

Scripts Are Relatively Short

If you're going to explore long-form narrative writing, it's nice to be able to finish a project in 3-6 months instead of 1-2 years.

Money

Thanks to a vigorous union, screenwriting can pay better than almost any other form of creative writing. If you are **very** good and **very** lucky, you might get some of that.

Magic

Screen stories are still (for now) the primary narrative medium of our time, the carrier of our myths, a common currency of our culture. There is a unique magic to the blending of image and sound, the capture of reality in the form of an imaginative dream.

Search your soul. Consider trying to write fiction instead -- or a graphic novel, a play, a videogame, a poem, an opera.

If you still want to write scripts -- turn the page.

BASIC PRINCIPLES

THERE IS NO PATH

There is no program you must attend or test you must pass before you can be an artist. There are certainly schools. Many are valuable.

But they're not required. Plenty of artists do just fine without them.

It's worth checking out as many books, videos, classes or podcasts as you can, taking from them what helps you.

But you can write without them. (Even this one.)

You can't just follow rules. There are too many, they change, and there is no actual authority.

And while you should study the work and careers of artists you admire, you can't follow their path. You are not them, and the world they worked in no longer exists.

The terrifying truth:

you are an artist if you make art

you make your way
using what you have
and being who you are
doing the best you can

If it's any comfort: every artist you admire had to do that, too.

figure out who you are
how you work
what you want to do
what you can do

explore your art and your world

ask questions and make choices

do the work, get projects done, and show them to people

and then do all that again...and again

EVERYTHING IS A CHOICE
&
EVERY CHOICE HAS A PRICE

Every scene idea or line of dialogue, every career problem that feels so complicated, overwhelming and scary...is in fact: a choice you face.

When you're writing, it's very hard to escape the feeling that "right answer" or the finished work is out there somewhere, waiting for you to get to it.

It's not.

You are creating your script, which does not exist yet, by making choices.

Being an artist is not about "getting it right," but about understanding the worth and consequences of possible paths and living with the fact that:

making art
is
making choices

Each choice may require you to weigh the needs of the project, the expectations of the genre, the needs of your collaborators, the reality of the marketplace, the values of your community.

But it must also come from you: the things you want to say, your desire to imitate a great artistic experience or to break free of a convention, your experiences and feelings.

And with any choice, there is a price.

If you add an exterior scene in the rain at night, you increase the budget. If you write a feature with no franchise or merchandising possibilities, you decrease the chances a big studio will want the project.

Often the creative price is simply the loss of all the other possibilities: once you give a character a specific job or background or relationship, you narrow some of the things they can do.

Every choice limits your options -- but also gives you new material to use, and a clearer sense of the work itself.

Recognizing that creative work is a process of making choices is liberating and empowering.

But it is not easy to make so many choices, so continually. Making choices is a skill. It takes practice to get good at it.

Start now.

WHAT YOU NEED MOST IS A TOOL BOX

For a plumber, every job is different. There is no ideal plumbing formula to follow. Sometimes a pipe must be made to connect the water main in the street with a bathroom on the second floor, but on another job a leaking joint must be replaced.

So a plumber has to be familiar with all the different types of pipes and valves and tools, and how they work.

Then the specifics of each task determine which tools or skills will be needed to get the job done.

An artist would do well to approach work like a plumber.

WRITE IT DOWN

Get into the habit of writing things down.

That sounds obvious, but it is the real core of all serious writing.

Don't wait until you know what you want to say. Get used to figuring that out **by writing**. Think on the page.

It doesn't matter how: carry a pen and a pocket notebook, or type into your phone.

Tell yourself the story on the page. Ask yourself questions in writing. Answer them in writing.

Get it out of your head. Get comfortable with capturing thought and feeling, putting things into words.

Practice jotting notes. It's not as easy as it looks, it takes you out of the moment. Learn to live with that, to make the transitions in and out swiftly and easily.

Moments of inspiration are brief. When you have one, it seems inconceivable that you will not remember, that the freshness and texture and power will fade. But they do.

The value of making writing a habit is you'll be able to capture magic when you run into it.

Want to be a writer? **Write it down.**

PROCESS

"METHOD" WRITING

"Method acting" was invented to deal with the fact that actors have to bring emotions on command -- while standing in front of a crowd, wearing unnatural makeup and someone else's clothing, saying words they've memorized about a life that isn't theirs.

Luckily for writers, mostly we can work in private -- but we also have to summon up emotions and creativity on command. For a lot of characters. And since you can't write a long narrative in one sitting, we have to be able to set it aside and come back to it. And most terrifying of all: an actor at least has a script to work from, while a writer faces a blank page.

But actors are the ones who figured out that:

**if you put your energy & focus
into the PROCESS,
you can make this
magical-mystery thing we do
even kind of...reliable**

Many method acting techniques do not apply to writing, but the basic **approach** is really important:

Focus On Process, Not Results
Don't try to control how the work will be received or try to match a planned external appearance. Just work on what you're doing and how you're doing it.

Focus On Characters Taking Action
Explore the reality and needs of the people in the story and discover what the moment is.

Be Specific

Creative work breaks down into finite, particular tasks. Even if you're stirring a universal feeling or coming up with a grand theme, you need to put that into a specific statement or question in a specific situation.

Moment to moment, line by line. These characters in these scenes.

Be In The Moment

Don't worry about what you're going to do later or how you got here. Connect to the given circumstances of the characters in this particular moment in the story.

And most important:

Use a Mechanical Process To Get To The Magic

Build a process that is so routine and practical you don't even think about it. It should be like walking or speaking: you do it until you're not thinking about the steps or the words, you're thinking about where you're going or what you're saying.

CREATE A RITUAL

A ritual is a set of things-to-do.

We tend to think of rituals as religious or mystical because a long time ago human beings figured out you can't **make** supernatural or spiritual things happen -- all you can do is create the conditions in which they're likely.

That's also how creativity works. You can't make it happen. All you can do is perform the actions that open you up to the magic.

If you don't like the notion of "magic," look at it scientifically:

anxiety prevents creativity
familiarity reduces anxiety
a ritual makes writing familiar

The distance between your mind and the page can seem terrifying. The goal of a ritual is to make it a well-worn path, a regular commute.

Ernest Hemingway sharpened a dozen pencils.

Vladimir Nabokov wrote novels on index cards.

Alex Haley took trips on a cargo freighter in order to write at sea.

Georges Simenon built a house in his backyard for writing. He would go in and not come out until a book was done. (He wrote short novels.)

John Cheever would get dressed in a business suit, take the elevator down to the basement of his apartment building, where he had rented a room to work in. He then took off the suit and sat in his underwear (because his workspace was next to the boiler room) and tied himself to his chair.

I don't think you should do any of that. The point: a writing ritual has to be personal.

Don't think about how it looks, about "should" or "right" or "recommended." Pay attention to your own experience.

Try To Make Part Of It Physical
A ritual should get you out of your head. Scribbling randomly on a piece of paper, cleaning your desk, stretching or exercising or meditating, even just opening a folder and closing all the other windows on your device.

Focus On The Work
Watching movies or even reading how-to-books are not good writing rituals. The process is about you, in this moment, being with your work.

It Should Be Within Your Control
Try not to make it dependent on getting a certain seat in your favorite cafe, or writing in a particular and hard-to-get type of notebook. (Or if you do, because it's working -- be ready to replace it if necessary.)

Make it small, simple, easy. Something you can own and carry with you. Something you can do right now and every day.

Your Process Should Not Be Dependent On Mood
It **creates** the mood.

Make It Something You Can Do By Yourself
Groups, clubs and meetings can be great, but try to build a ritual that doesn't depend on others being available. (If you work with a partner, build a ritual together.)

Work With Your Reality
Don't try to bend your life to fit your ritual. It should fit into your life.

And if your reality changes, adapt your ritual.

Your Process Should Not Harm You
It should not leave you injured or sick, bring you into conflict with people in your life, or cost more than you can afford. It should not involve drugs or alcohol, no matter how mythic that cliche seems.

Build It Through Trial & Error
You'll need to test different versions to find one that works. You'll know it does if you:

> find yourself (after a time) becoming more confident when you do it
>
> get work done
>
> begin to look forward to it, or at least feel some faith that if you follow it -- even when you feel nothing or worse -- it works

Give It Time
A lot of what makes a ritual work is repetition. Sometimes you know instantly that something is not working -- but do try to give your explorations and trials a chance. If you're not absolutely sure, give it time to settle in and work.

You can't **make** creativity happen.

All you can do is create a set of circumstances -- a ritual -- that makes lightning more likely to strike, and helps you use the inspiration when it shows up.

SMALL STEPS

**there is no other way
to make a journey of a thousand miles
than one step at a time**

You may feel you already know this, but it has nothing to do with knowing. Small steps are a tool, like a sponge or a flashlight. You can't just say *"ah yes, I know about that flashlight..."* and expect to see any better.

it only works if you use it

"I want to be really good, even exceptional, so I can't be messing around with small steps."
Small steps are how you get really good. Greatness requires practice: making each small step a little better, over and over (and over.)

"Small steps are not enough."
That's like saying you don't want to be paid in dollars because a dollar isn't very much money.

"Small steps will take too long."
Do not discount the momentum you get from accomplishing absolutely **anything**. Even the smallest, dumbest accomplishment gives you a boost of focus and power.

So -- let's talk about how:

Choose Your "Unit"
Find a specific measurable unit of progress. I don't personally believe time is a good measure: we all know what it's like to put in hours and get nowhere.

A good way to figure out your units is -- at any given step, ask:

what are you trying to DO?

work out the plot?

make an outline?

write a first draft?

what is that MADE OF?

a plot is made of **events**

an outline is made of **scenes**

a draft is made of **sentences**

That's your unit: the thing that what-you're-trying-to-do is **made of.**

Do ONE Of Those

one event in your story

one scene in your outline

one rough-draft sentence

Start Micro
If the step is small enough, you can make yourself do it.
Start with a really small unit, even just one sentence a day.

Any amount is okay, except zero.

It may feel a little foolish, but that's better than the usual hash of shame and guilt and ridiculous expectations.

Don't make the day's work too big to carry.

The point is to gain confidence, to gain skills, to get familiar.

You May Have To Force Yourself For A While
Even tiny steps can be unexpectedly hard to take. You will not feel like it. You will find a billion excuses not to do it.

SLOWLY Increase It
Stick with doing that one step every day for a while. Then slowly add more.

This is not infinite! You can't just add and add. You'll discover -- with experience and practice -- a natural average amount you can do in a work session. That's your step. Keep taking that step, every day.

Setting yourself too big a step and failing or doing it badly can really discourage you. (**Falsely**! because you failed at trying to accomplish an impossible task.)

If One Of Your Small Steps Gets Bigger -- Let It
Sometimes you get on a roll -- you want to keep working past your step. Go with that! But then the next day, start small again. The small step is your base line, your minimum daily requirement.

The magic: when you keep taking small steps -- you get confident, you find your rhythm. You get things done. You begin to look forward to it.

Will this make the work great? Will it solve all your problems? Yes! Because work can't be great if you don't **do** it. And you can't solve problems if you're still trying to figure out how to get started.

This is how you get started.

A PROCESS OF QUESTIONS

The simplest, most reliable process for creative writing:

**write down a question
and then
write down the answer**

When you see the questions and answers on a page, you tend to work in a more specific, concrete way.

Whatever answer you have, the best you can do at that moment: make a choice and write it down.

If you're not ready to do that yet: write down **possible** answers.

If your answer is not something you can add to an outline and write as a scene: ask more questions, until it is.

Write that into the outline.

Then ask more questions, about that answer. Write down more answers.

Do this again and again, until you know what's happening in every moment of the story. The goal is to grope your way toward moments, actions that become scenes.

Eventually you get to the very last question:

"which words should I use to write this scene?"

And the answer to **that** one is...you write the script.

Okay, so then: what exactly are these questions you're supposed to ask?

Start with the classics:

who

what

where

when

why

Other Useful Questions
"The 6 Essential Questions."

who is it about?

what do they want?

why can't they get it?

what do they do about that?

why doesn't that work?

how does it end?

What Is The Scene?

how is that idea or moment going to be a scene?

what is the purpose of this scene?

what is the central dramatic action of this scene?

what do the characters want to accomplish in the scene?

why do they want that?

how do they want to accomplish it?

what action begins the scene?

what action ends the scene?

where does it take place?

does this scene fulfill an expectation of the genre?

is this the most interesting, emotional, original or exciting version of this scene?

what is the tension of this scene: what are we hoping for, what do we fear?

Is It Specific?

The more specific your choices, the more powerfully your writing works. You cannot get too specific.

Is It Simple?

Screen stories live intensely in the moment. They can't stay still and they can't go back. In each moment, the audience can only focus on so much.

Simple means you know what matters in this moment.

Simple does not mean easy or shallow. It does not rule out ambiguity or layers of meaning. Complexity is the combination of simple things.

What Changes?

Someone is **doing** something in a scene. What happens when they do it? Do they get what they want, or not? Either way: something changes.

Sometimes change happens between scenes. Or perhaps the new thing is routine to the characters but new to the audience.

This is also a reminder to mix it up: if you've been indoors, get out. If you've had a chase, lock your characters in an elevator. Vary your sentence structure.

How Do We Know That?

One of the key problems of screenwriting. The means by which a script or a screen can convey ideas and information are ridiculously limited.

how will the audience know whatever it is that you want in the story?

what **action** or **scene** or **line** reveals that to us? How?

Why Now?
People act or speak for a reason. What has happened to make a character take an action or make a decision or say a line in this moment?

What Is It Like For Them?
Forget what the audience needs to know, or what other shows or movies did. It's just the character, in this moment.

what is it like for them?

what do they see, taste, smell?

what are they thinking?

what are they feeling?

what do they need?

what do they want to do?

Can I Cut it?
If this bit didn't exist: what would not happen, what would not make sense?

Some stuff is delightful and you leave it in just because. But most often, if you **can** cut something...you probably should.

This question also reveals those few moments you **cannot** cut: it shows you what needs to be absolutely protected, no matter what else has to change to keep it.

No matter how new or hard a project is, this process gives you one reliable, reassuring, confidence-building thought:

at least I know what to do now: ask questions

USE WHAT YOU HAVE

This is so simple, it's easy to underestimate:

**once you've made ANY choice
you can USE THAT
to make the next one**

Suppose all you've got is a premise:

```
an identity thief and their victim fall in
love
```

That's a fine idea, but you still need over a hundred more pages of detail before you've got a script, which is a bit intimidating. So look at what you have.

In this **one sentence** you've already made **four choices**. You've got two people:

```
an identity thief

their victim
```

-- and two actions:

```
stealing identities

falling in love
```

So you've already got four things to work with. Let's look at just **one:**

```
an identity thief
```

A thief takes stuff from other people. What does that tell us about this character? Just a few possibilities:

```
they don't care about the law -- they feel
they are above it
```

```
they don't care about the law -- they feel
like an outsider or outcast

they have a good reason or a noble plan

they're okay with harming others because
they're desperate or damaged

they don't realize how much they harm others
```

But they're not just a thief, they're an **identity** thief: no armed robbery or smash-and-grab for them. So:

```
they're relatively smart (or have been trained
by someone who is)

what they do is at a distance, likely online
```

Ah! From that - we have something new: these two people probably don't live in the same place.

Which means: one of them is, eventually, going to have to go to the other.

Which one? Why?

That also means we have two **more** things: the places they are from. If one lives in a trailer in the desert, that's going to be a different person with a different life than someone sharing an apartment in a big city with three other people.

Look at all the material we've got, from one simple sentence. (And we haven't even gotten to the most interesting bit: the falling-in-love part. How? Why?)

But what happens when you can't "Use What You Have" because you **can't think of anything?**

"Use What You Have" also implies something very important:

you always have SOMETHING

Most of "I can't think of anything" is actually:

*I don't **like** what I have*

*I don't **trust** it*

*I don't think it's **good enough***

To that I still say: **use what you have.**

start from where you are
work with what you've got

Use it **even if** you don't like it. Use it anyway. Use it as a start.

Then ask: what **exactly** is bad about it? Too short, too long? It's cliche? It's vague?

Use that: there's an opposite to any bad thing. Work on making it a little bit of the opposite. You don't have to make it good -- it's nice, but it's not required. Just make it distinctly not-as-bad.

If you really truly can't think of **any reason** to make one choice over another: make a random choice. Now you have something to work with.

Finally: to use what you have, you have to **know** what you have.

put WHATEVER you have into
words, on a page

You can't hate it and tear it apart -- and make it better -- unless it's there.

you always have SOMETHING

once you've made ANY choice

you can use THAT

to make the next one

use what you have

THE SPIRAL PROCESS

When you conceive of writing, you probably think of it like this:

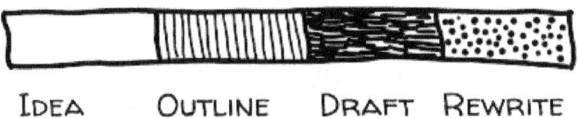

...or maybe this:

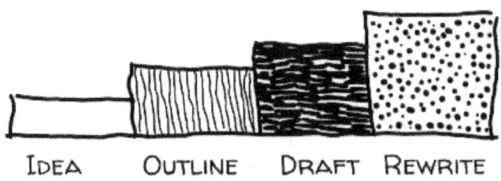

But it's really this:

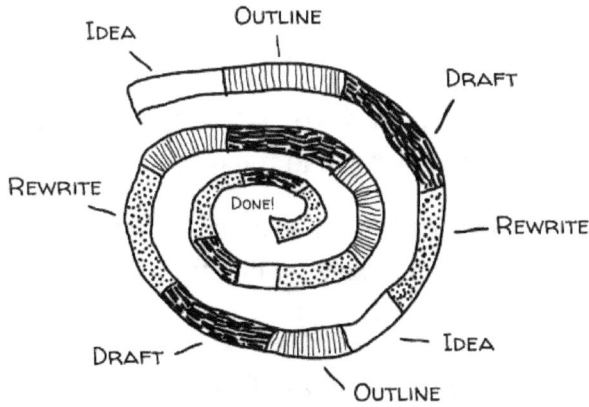

The "non-spiral" versions suggest that we get one part done and then move on to the next.

But artists discover things as they work. There are questions or problems you can't see yet, things you learn or invent as you write, that will change the project.

Every time you sit down to write, you are slightly different. You did stuff since you last wrote, things happened in the world. So you work with slightly new eyes each time.

A straight line also implies marching toward a fixed, stable destination. But the finished work does not exist yet. When you make choices, you define what that center, that finished work, will be.

Looking at your work process as a spiral lets you use all that to make the work better: keep coming around, looking at it with different eyes, improving or solving a different little bit each time.

Especially for those of us who tend to overthink: a spiral process is the best way I know to cope with too many ideas, too many fears, the complexity of the task. It lets you skip steps that aren't working, keep learning and then come back.

nobody gets it all at once

You do the best you can at any given moment. You get a rough version, an incomplete version, you try things -- because you know: I'll get back to this later and make it better.

If you just make it **a little better** -- come up with **one** inspired bit, each time through -- those new bits will show you what to do next.

So leave room in your process to go back or around and keep re-approaching everything.

When you do that enough, it all begins get really good.

HOW DO YOU START?

Start where you are. Use what you have.

You've got a:

    beginning

    ending

    genre

    plot twist

    what-if

    character

    line of dialogue

    memory

    observation

    message

    topic

    world

    feeling

That's where you start. Write it down. Whatever it is.

Then ask questions. Get specific. Think in scenes.

No matter where you start, eventually you'll have to take all the steps, fill in all the missing pieces, create characters, scenes and story. So just take some first steps and figure it out from there.

All creative work begins with some initial spark, some element that hooks the artist. It may not turn out to be the heart of the work, it may even eventually be discarded --that's fine. Give it fuel and let it cook.

HOW DO I KNOW AN IDEA IS GOOD?

In my opinion, there is no such thing as a bad idea for a story.

Your job is to **make** it good.

Some ideas **are** more (or less) likely to sell at a given moment in a given market. That's a separate question. To answer that, study that market.

Certainly some ideas present challenges: it would be difficult to tell a story narrated by a character who speaks gibberish, or to watch a single character talk to the camera for two hours -- but the work of figuring out how to give the audience a good dramatic experience within those limits might produce something original and excellent.

What If It Has Been Done Before?
Everything has been done before.

"It's been done," is an executive's reason to pass -- but having-been-done-before-successfully is also a prime reason The Industry makes anything. Go figure.

What is **your** version? What are you bringing that's different?

Do that.

A Note On Adapting Books, Comics, Plays And True Stories
Do not do this unless you have a legal document giving you the right to do so.

No matter how big a fan you are, or how great it could be, or how much you believe you can win over the rights holder once they see your script. If you have access to the rights-owner and can negotiate a written legal contract...sure, why not. But otherwise: only write what you own.

If the work is in the public domain: feel free.

(If you want to know more about "rights" and "public domain": research with legitimate legal authorities. I am not a lawyer and this is not legal advice!)

IS THIS WORTH WRITING?

In making this calculation, most people are actually asking:

how hard will it be?

will it be something I can make money from?

The answers are pretty simple:

it will be harder than you expect.

you are very unlikely to make money from it.

But those aren't really the right questions. The real question is:

what do you want to get out of writing a script?

Among realistic goals:

see if you can do it

learn

improve your skills (plotting, writing dialogue, etc)

do something you enjoy

give yourself something to direct or act in

create something you imagine and see what it turns out
to be

Among unrealistic goals:

get rich or famous

get someone to love you

get that thing you imagine exactly into a movie

show everyone that you are better than they are

get to hang around with famous people

There is no way to know how good something will be until you write it and show it to people.

You can't control what other people will think or feel.

There is no script "so good" it sells -- as the endless stories of brilliant scripts going unsold will attest. Many factors other than quality decide whether a script sells.

Write a script you want to see. Choose a story that thrills or amuses or scares or touches you.

Choose a project you want to spend time with, because you will.

Choose something that you will be glad to have written even if it fails.

Write it the best you can. That's all anyone can do, and the only way to get better.

BRAINSTORMING

If writing is slow or painful, it may partly be because you're not comfortable with brainstorming.

Every time you write, you're actually doing little "micro brainstorms." You face a blank page, or a blank spot in your story, and try to come up with possibilities.

Luckily, brainstorming is a skill -- which means if you work on it, you can get better.

The first and most important thing to know:

brainstorm on the page

Maybe you **can** do it in your head, but something about writing it down makes a difference. You get to see your thoughts as concrete things you can play with and use.

seriously:
WRITE IT DOWN

Next: brainstorming is not just free-associating random thoughts. (The technical term for that is "procrastinating.")

brainstorming is thinking
in a very loose, creative way
ABOUT a SPECIFIC question

```
"How does she steal the diamond?"
"What things might happen in a western?"
"What does she answer when he says that?"
```

**within that specific "arena":
pay attention to
whatever comes into your head**

DO NOT EDIT OR CRITICIZE

if nothing comes: GET MORE SPECIFIC

Sometimes just choose one word in the question and focus on that:

```
How does she steal the diamond?
```

Think about ways to "steal" :

```
grabs it

smashes something

swallows it

makes it vanish

makes it appear to vanish

magic

illusion

distraction

takes a hostage

sets fire to the building

puts it in a glass of water

uses chewing gum

replaces it with a duplicate

waits until they're transporting it

cracks the safe

seduces the owner
```

```
hypnotizes everyone in the room
convinces them it's worthless
```

Include The Obviously Bad Ideas
Get stupid! Write down all your outrageously bad ideas during brainstorm sessions, no matter how clear it is they're not gonna work. Get comfortable with accepting them, treating them like any other idea.

You can always throw them away later, but they open new paths.

Refuse To Judge
Start to notice when you think:

> *that's bad*
>
> *that won't work*
>
> *they won't like this*
>
> *I'll be judged*

Get in the habit of looking out for that negative inner voice. It is cowardly: when caught, it slinks back into its creepy cave.

In order to do all this, you must:

Let Go Of Control.
Which is **not** easy.

Our brains are constantly sorting, prioritizing and defending-against thoughts. It happens so fast we're not even aware of it -- but without this layer of resistance we would immediately overload.

Alas, as with many survival instincts (like fight-or-flight) it's not always helpful when you're trying to do something other than survive.

The silver lining: if your brain is constantly sorting and discarding stuff, that means all these thoughts are already there. Your brain is working away all the time, exploring, creating, inventing.

You just have to stop it from instinctively clamping down and swatting that creativity away.

The way to get good at that is, as with any skill:

PRACTICE
brainstorming
letting go
refusing to judge

do EASY versions

take small steps

keep the pressure & stakes low
look into relaxation and
the psychological concept of "flow"

do it often

give this TIME
work on it, now and then, for months

This is not about willpower. It's about small steps, done repeatedly, casually, with low pressure.

No One Is Watching: Entertain Yourself!
This is a **private** process, just for you. So have fun. Don'tworry about what anyone else would think about what you're doing.

This is not about willpower. It's about small steps, done repeatedly, casually, with low pressure.

No One Is Watching: Entertain Yourself!
This is a **private** process, just for you. So have fun. Don't worry about what anyone else would think about what you're doing.

Try Opposites
Sometimes thinking about the reverse of what you're looking for can bring new things to mind. Like in our example: how do you protect a diamond from being stolen?

Don't Worry About Being Unique Or Original
How did other movies and shows do this? How do people do this in real life?

You can't just copy them, but when you're brainstorming you can start with borrowed stuff and then mess with it to make it new, make it yours.

Step Away And Come Back Later
There is no rule you have to do this all at once. It's not a stunt, you're not showing anyone how much you can throw down.

Know When To Stop
No one is going to give you a prize for most brainstormed items. You're only going to use one.

Look at what you've got, see how these new ideas might work.

After a while: stop brainstorming...and start writing.

NOBODY GETS IT ALL AT ONCE

Writing takes time.

We get interrupted. We have to do other things. We don't think everything out perfectly. And sometimes the words just don't come.

Many writers try to rush through, hoping to avoid pain: the running-over-hot-coals theory.

There are no coals.

This kind of work builds, it accumulates. Enjoy the process.

Every writer's life makes different demands, every brain works differently. Get to know your own, don't set goals or plans based on some ideal or other person.

Try to build a process that allows you to take the time it takes.

SCRAP PILES

A good amount of writing happens when you're not writing. Stuff comes to you all the time.

Get into the habit of writing it down and putting it somewhere so you can use it later.

A Place For Everything And Everything In Its Place
Workshops -- whether for artists or auto mechanics -- tend to have lots of specialized cabinets or shelves with little bins or big flat drawers: specific places designed to hold the raw materials of their work.

You need a digital or paper version of that. Make a set of folders or documents sorted into categories, so you have somewhere to put things when you jot them down -- and can find them later.

Some possible scrap pile categories:

> *story ideas*
>
> *events & bits*
>
> *characters*
>
> *places*
>
> *jobs*
>
> *themes*
>
> *bits of dialogue*
>
> *names*
>
> *observations*
>
> *descriptions*
>
> *things overheard*
>
> *quotes*
>
> *clippings*

It takes time, but after a while you'll have a collection of interesting stuff that might come in handy.

The secret power of scrap piles is: even if you never use the stuff in them, they still help you write.

**ideas come to you
more often & more easily
when you get in the habit
of writing everthing down**

When you make a scrap pile, you begin noticing more, thinking of more, capturing more.

And that's worth doing.

LEARN HOW TO WRITE BADLY

No amount of planning will let you skip the step where you set down stuff that isn't right yet.

No matter how much you theorize and analyze, there are going to be questions you never think of until you set it down in words.

The first steps are almost always a mess. You're just marking out the shape, giving it form, getting the feel, finding the voice.

So throw down whatever you can, even if it is absolute junk.

I have heard it called "the vomit draft," which is kind of accurate, but...eww. I prefer "rough draft."

Try things. Guess. Explore. Write it fast, loose, sketchy, incomplete, approximate. **Never** think of showing it to anyone. Don't look back, keep writing new material.

You will suffer waves of uncertainty and vulnerability while grinding out those first rough scenes. But once you truly believe in the process, you can march through the fog and darkness, confident of one thing: you will not fall off the edge of the world.

It's going to be awful. Clumsy, on-the-nose, disorganized, vague, weak.

But in the middle of all that garbage, you will write something -- maybe just a sentence, maybe a whole scene -- that contains glints of gold. Something that will be good when it is polished and refined.

Keep going. Get it all done, then step away, put it aside for a bit.

When you look at it again: the work is there, asking for help. It lets you start to see what it is. You see connections, causes, effects, relationships. Blank spots that need to be filled-in.

It's hard to write knowing that you're not really getting it.

But if you can get used to writing badly, then you'll write.

LEARN TO LOVE THE LIMITS

When you begin a project it can go anywhere, be anything, be everything.

But it isn't entirely real until you admit that no matter how dense, epic or complex it may be -- it is still made up of a limited number of scenes, pages, words. Some characters and ideas will be more important than others.

And the reverse is true, too -- if you don't feel you can come up with enough: it's only a limited amount, one bit at a time you can get there.

Once you've set some limits, each chosen element within the boundaries becomes an anchor, a landmark. It becomes the "what you have" in "use what you have."

Limits give you confidence. They become a way to make choices and discover values.

There should come a moment when you see the piece of work not as potential and vast, but as narrow and possible.

FORCING YOURSELF TO WRITE

I often have to force myself to write. I never think I am "ready." I prefer to theorize, analyze, plan, research...anything but face the task of putting words on a page.

It helps to not think of it as "force" but instead as "discipline" -- which can simply mean having a method, a process, a way of getting things done.

We have become so used to the negative meanings of "discipline" -- punishment, oppression -- that we forget its beautiful and noble version: a field of interest, a devotion to the rituals of a pursuit.

Without some discipline, it is unlikely you can be a professional writer. Even if you can manage to get your original work done by riding waves of feeling -- the business of writing includes deadlines, changes-on-demand and collaboration.

But even just for yourself: it is worthwhile to stop thinking of discipline as something imposed or punitive.

When done properly, it is a comfort and a pleasure.

Practice writing when you don't want to, and writing things you don't want to write.

Do it a little bit at a time, over and over, privately, when no one is looking and it can't hurt.

It's often by a certain amount of drudgery that you come to live inside the world of the work.

REWRITING

For most new writers, rewriting is just proofreading -- or starting again from scratch.

But when you finish a draft, you don't then just march through the text "correcting" it. You're still writing it, often discovering whole new aspects and layers.

**rewriting is not
an extra step you do after writing**

it is PART of writing

Most writers I know don't even feel like they fully understand their own project until they've read the first draft and started to rewrite it.

There is no "right way" to rewrite. If your way of working is working: do that.

These are just some tools and approaches you can try if it's not working.

My First Step: Just Read Through
Ideally, don't stop -- try to get the flow, the story experience. (Although, honestly, most writers can't help marking it up a little or jotting notes.)

Be aware: it is **hard** to read your own writing.

Not only because you're emotionally fragile (though that's a very real thing) but because you honestly can't see it. It's too familiar, you know what you intended, there's some weird perceptual malfunction.

So, often you need to kind-of trick yourself -- the way painters look at their work in a mirror.

**do anything you can
to LOOK AT YOUR WORK
WITH FRESH EYES:**

print it
change the font
read it on a different device
read it in a different room.

Then: don't just go back to page one and start "fixing it" line-by-line yet.

Stop and think about the big picture: story, characters, style, vision.

How much of what you thought you were doing is there in this thing you read?

Get to know this thing: it's an actual text now. Try to **see** it: not what it's **supposed** to be, not what you **wanted** it to be.

**there IS NO finished work out there
waiting for you to get to it --
there's just the best version of
what it actually is**

Part of creating something is discovering what it is. You're trying to figure out what you like in what you've got. You can't do that if you keep starting over again, nor if all you're doing is looking for what's "wrong."

This is really important:

work from what's GOOD

Yes, some of it will be awful -- but somewhere in all that, you will find something unique or smart or emotional...**something** you like.

Learn to look for what you've done that is even just **near** what you like, and use that to anchor you and steer by. (I know: "anchor" and "steer" are conflicting images -- but they're both true here.)

> **examine every negative note or thought**
> **& figure out**
> **the constructive step it gives you**

Use The Outline
The outline is not just a stage you pass through before you write -- it's an ongoing way to work. It's a place to note anything you need to do, to talk to yourself and figure things out.

Get used to moving back and forth between outline and text. It's two ways of thinking -- and you never stop using either one.

(If you don't want to make or use an outline, that's fine -- just have **somewhere** that you can write and think in an "eye in the sky" way, instead of down in the weeds of the words.)

Copy And "Conform" The Outline
To keep working with your outline: **make a new copy** -- archive the old one.

Then go through the script again scene by scene, changing the outline to match it. Delete anything in the outline that is already done.

Create A Things-To-Do List
Go through the script again and note what's not working and (if you know) what needs to be done.

Don't trust yourself to know later what you see now. Write it down.

Ask yourself what each scene is really about. There's no point correcting the words in a scene that doesn't work. If you see a line you want to fix, fix it -- but the most important thing to get a grip on is: the story and the characters.

what is the point/purpose of this scene?

who is doing what?

what do they want?

what is the action?

what is the change, or news, or development?

Break The Work Down Into Small Tasks
Work on one scene at a time. If you can't figure out how to fix something -- move on, and fix everything else.

Stay Specific
Too long. Too fast. Too on the nose. Not enough detail. Too much detail. Gives away too much. Character is focused on the wrong thing. He's too angry. She's not curious enough. Etc, etc.

Let Things Go -- For A Reason
Many people misunderstand the cliche "kill your darlings" to mean, *if you like something in your work, get rid of it.* That's ridiculous. It means: *if you have a good reason to take something out --* **even if you love it, let it go.**

Part of rewriting is throwing out some of your work. That can be hard. Let yourself feel it, mourn your losses.

If it helps, put things you like but had to cut into a separate document. Later, you can look at them and maybe even return some to the script...but most of the time, once they're gone for a while, you can live without them.

Focus On The Script -- Not On Yourself

You are judging this specific work, not your talent or future.

Explore, Experiment

Learn to accept what professionals know from experience:

**everything you write
can be done
many different ways**

So try stuff out, see what it's like if you do it a different way.

Passes

One way to think of rewriting is the concept of "passes." Every time you go through the script and change things, it's a "pass."

In each pass you can focus on a specific element. It is not always helpful to just go over and over the script with the same focus and frame-of-mind.

Instead, sometimes go through it tracking a particular character's "arc," or looking closely at the dialogue, or scene descriptions or action scenes.

The End Of Rewriting

Each time you go through it, the list of things to work on will be shorter. After a while you are just "polishing": small or superficial changes.

And one day, you realize you've done the best you can. It's not perfect, but it's as good as you can make it.

You may never stop seeing stuff that needs fixing -- but after a while: stop.

Show it to people, see what they get and what they don't.

And then you'll probably rewrite it again.

RESEARCH

Research can be a marvelous well-spring of texture and ideas. It can also be a mire of quicksand that sucks you in and destroys you.

Do You Need To Do Research?
If you're writing about something you've experienced personally -- or something entirely made-up: maybe not. But most creative writing falls somewhere in between those, and research can help.

Research For Creative Writing
In academic or scientific research, you're trying to provide a formal, documented path to support what you're saying-- but research for creative writing is just an invisible well of inspiration and texture. It's about understanding your characters and the world they live in.

So there really are no rules. Anything goes -- which sounds fun until somebody loses an eye. Or a lawsuit.

Therefore, this is **really important:**

Keep Your Research SEPARATE From Your Writing
Writing is a long complicated process. It is easy to forget what you researched, and then use someone else's words -- which is a serious problem.

So put your research work in different documents, different folders from what you are writing. Use a different font or color.

Make sure you can tell what you researched from what you wrote.

Collect Your Research In An Organized Method

You can't use it if you don't put it somewhere that you can find later.

Don't just pile it up in a "junk drawer." Gather your research in such a way that the relevant, inspiring, useful "bits" can be pulled out and turned into the stuff of your work.

The Internet

The good news: we are living in a golden age of research. There is so much access to so much information.

The bad news: the internet is a gigantic indiscriminate pile of everything and a lot of it is garbage.

Many internet sources present opinions as facts, or just copy and paste stuff they found online. Please educate yourself about how to safely and wisely gather information from the internet. (You can find many articles about that...alas, on the internet.)

In general: try to look for people sharing their personal experiences. It is astonishing how many people post about their lives, their jobs, their homes -- a huge trove of raw authentic material. You can see what food restaurants serve, attend birthday parties in someone's backyard, walk along a street on the other side of the world.

Books And Libraries

For most of the past few centuries, people put information in books. Books are often more reliable than internet articles: they mostly had editors and publishers with lawyers, who did some fact-checking.

The contents of **many books** are **not** on the internet.

Learn how to use libraries, and how to buy used books (which can be quite cheap...on the internet.)

IRL

If possible, try going to a place like the one you are writing about, or talking to people who do a thing your characters do.

"Research" Relevant Movies And Shows

If you're working on a western -- watch a lot of westerns! If you're working on a story about a **topic** or a **time** or a **place**: take a deep dive into all sorts of movies or shows or stories about that. Even the really bad ones can stir up useful ideas.

Limit Your Research

There's too much stuff out there. To avoid spending your whole life just researching:

Use Your Story

You're weaving this knowledge into a narrative. Use that to help figure out which stuff will be of use, and which is just fascinating but...extra.

Your main priority: does this help me with my characters or story?

Wander Through The Junk Pile Of Knowledge With A Goal

Narrow your search in any research session. Choose a particular aspect of your topic for that day's work.

Skim Until You Strike Gold

You're not going to be tested about this stuff later. You don't need to know everything.

Do Not Put Off Writing To Do Research

Characters and story **are** shaped by research, but that is an ongoing process.

Work on the characters and story, first and foremost. Do that work, find that stuff, make those choices. Then your research will have a meaningful place to go.

In general:

**write first,
research after
(or at least during)**

How Much Research Is Too Much?

Every artist -- and every project -- is different. Are you getting your creative work done? Decide from there.

But just to give you an important reality check -- FYI:

The Entertainment Industry DOES NOT CARE About Research

Your research will be at the mercy of a business that wants characters with perfect teeth in the Middle Ages, or a tax advantage that moves your Louisiana bayou drama to Salt Lake City.

Literally hundreds of people may change the details of your script, based on their taste or budget or product placement deals.

**the really valuable research
is the stuff that gets deep inside,
woven invisibly, emotionally
into the people, the scenes, the story**

Think about what is essential, emotional and narrative about your researched reality -- and then make up something that is **yours**, using those details.

**research for creative writing is about
finding raw material
which you must TRANSFORM
into something NEW & YOUR OWN**

TAKE ART APART

Even if you already do a version of this, it can be useful to make it a conscious experiment or exercise:

Take your favorite movies or shows apart.

Look at them mechanically, figure out what they're made of, how they work.

I am not talking about studying books or videos or podcasts where some expert takes it apart for you. That's fine too, but what's important here is that you **take it apart by yourself.**

I don't know why this works, because it's trying to pull the magic right off of your favorite stuff. I think the trick is: while you **do** lose the "passive magic" of being an audience, you connect with the getting-your-hands-dirty "active magic" of making art.

Anyway -- it works, so let's get down to it:

Play some movie or episode of a show that you think is really good on a device that allows you to stop and start, along with some technology that allows you to write, and:

Write Out A List Of Every Scene
Hit pause whenever a scene changes, and write down what the last scene was about. Who was involved, what changed, what was the central action?

Essentially, make an outline of this thing you like. Think in scenes.

Then go through the same movie or episode again:

Choose A Specific Element To Study Each Time Through.

scene structure

dialogue

character

set pieces

exposition

pace

Focus On The Mechanics

For example, when looking at the dialogue:

do they use short sentences, or long?

do the characters have different ways of talking? How
is that done?

how much subtext, how much on-the-nose?

are there speeches? when, who, how, why?

Type Out Some Dialogue In Script Format

Even if you have a copy of the script, take a good scene and type
it out for yourself.

Get used to seeing these magical moments as the same basic
crap you write: a handful of words, typed in an ugly format.

Find A Copy Of The Script And Compare It

There are a lot of scripts available online. If the script for the
movie you want isn't available, choose another movie that you
can compare in this way.

Stop to read each scene after you watch it. Look at the
differences. Look at the art and craft of writing a script --
not making a movie.

Learn to separate scripts from finished movies. Take note of all the things in the finished film that you can't write: the way an actor says a line, the edits, the cinematography, music, locations, production design.

Read scripts for stuff you've seen. Read scripts for stuff you haven't seen. Read scripts that haven't been made (*The Black List* site is one place to look for these.)

Try taking apart something you can't stand, or a hit that you just don't get. (I have to warn you, this may lead to some grudging respect)

Some Ways to Identify Real Scripts Online
Search "screenplays PDF" or "(Title) Script PDF."

But beware: many online scripts are just **transcripts** of the finished film. I am not a fan of these, you can't learn much from them. You can spot these fairly easily: any script that's ever been made was changed during production. Actors don't always say the lines exactly as written. Locations, budget and other production realities require changes. Lines, and even scenes, get cut or rearranged during editing. **If the "script" you're reading** *exactly* **matches the finished film -- don't trust it.**

Useful indicators that a script is real:

a title page.

a date on the title page.

a production company or agent contact information, usually in the lower-left corner of the title page.

a list of "colored revisions" on the cover page (named things like "blue" "pink" "goldenrod" etc, each with a date.)

for 20th-century scripts: evidence that it is a xerox, including holes punched near the left margin, dirt on the page, crooked pages.

Many 21st-century PDF scripts are "for your consideration" versions, circulated during award seasons. These are legit -- albeit sometimes cleaned-up. They will have a company name on the title page and at least small differences from the finished film.

You Are NOT Looking For A Formula
This is **very important.** What you find doesn't have to be true of **every** movie or show (nothing is!) You take art apart to find how a particular script or story works and how that relates to what you're trying to do.

Think About How To Steal
You can't just do what they did, but you can steal their approach, mechanics and devices. Think about **your version** of what they do.

Taking art apart, by itself, will not teach you how to write. You still have to do your own work.

But it gives you all sorts of possibilities, ways to solve problems or accomplish things. It's stuff for your toolbox.

It also might help you get out from under the spell of great work, because that is a siren-song. Even the great works were, at some point, just work. The script is so much less than the movie or show, and it's important to get used to that.

Take some art apart and see how the magic is made out of crude basic elements of the action, the dialogue and your words on a page.

Those same elements you're working with.

WASTING TIME

Even when work is flowing perfectly, there will be moments when you look back at a section of work and realize: that was a waste of time.

Don't panic.

This is not the same as procrastination. Procrastination is not-doing-the-job.

Wasting time is doing the job badly, or in an unproductive direction -- which are sometimes required parts of the creative process.

Some Things That Are NOT A Waste Of Time

Testing And   A Possibility
A variety of versions of the same great quote, attributed to both Benjamin Franklin and Thomas Edison, all say essentially: *"I haven't failed. I have succeeded in proving these hundreds of ways to do this thing don't work."*

Doing Work That Doesn't Sell
Selling is not within your control.

Doing Work That Isn't As Good As You Hoped
It's **never** what you think it will be. Write it as well as you can, let it be as good as it is....and then do all that again. That's the job.

You don't want to **try** to waste time, but when you do -- don't beat yourself up.

If you find you have wasted time on something: look back
and see if the impulse you were following was familiar. If so:

does it **usually** waste time?

can you notice that impulse **sooner** next time, and stop?

(Then it wasn't a waste of time!)

WRITING OUT OF ORDER

Often you struggle with a script -- but eventually one bit works and you discover the voice of the project. It's a crucial moment. Everything gets a little easier.

Who says that has to be in the first pages?

This is not for everyone, and not all the time. But it can be a useful tool when you are jammed-up, frustrated or uninspired:

**you don't have to write your script
in order
from beginning to end**

There are good reasons to start on page one and work your way through to the end. In theory it puts you on the same journey as the audience, and if that works -- great. Always do what works.

But you're **not** on the same journey as the audience. You are wandering into places that **don't exist yet,** and by going there, you create them.

Some scenes are just begging to be written. They're the stylistic or thematic heart of the whole thing. Or the scene is an interesting challenge, a puzzle: *how're you gonna make **that** work?* Or it's just something cool, nifty, fun. Maybe it's just easier than most.

Why not jump into those?

This works best if you have an outline. *(I urge you to read my two chapters about outlines if you're anti-outline, outline challenged or outline-intolerant.)*

At some point you **do** need to work your way through the whole thing from start to finish. But how cool when you do that, to find you have some scenes already staked-out -- as if, on a long journey, you've gone ahead and set up campsites and left supplies along the way.

Sometimes when you get stuck, grinding isn't the only solution.

WORK BACKWARDS

When you can't figure out what happens next, or something's not working: try looking at where you want to end up.

For example: *at the end of this story, these people have to agree (or disagree).* Or: *at the end of this scene, the guy has to steal a pineapple.*

Some questions to ask:

> what am I trying to **get to**?
>
> why can't the characters get there right away?
>
> what does it take to get there?
>
> what obstacles are keeping them from getting there?
>
> if they do get there: what does that take, what do they have to do?
>
> if they don't get there: why not and what does that make them do next?

You can do this just in a scene, or for a character, or about the story as a whole.

It's a useful tool.

TAPPING THE CORE

When our process is not working, we often say: *I can't think of anything or I don't feel it.* It seems like our ability to think and feel is broken, or used up.

It's not.

I believe within each of us there are limitless reservoirs of pure feeling. This kind of core emotion is so powerful it can be overwhelming and scary -- so human nature has built-in all kinds of mental safety valves to keep us from just opening the floodgates or touching the third rail.

We can't just walk right up and plug into our feelings. But they **are** there.

Creativity seems to be like that, too: it's always there, you just have to learn how to get to it -- which is **not** by force, nor going directly at it.

Experiment with different methods to tap in again.

Often you just need to step away, do something different, let your inner safety-valves reset. Try things that have worked in the past, and if those don't work...try whatever else is unlikely, or even ridiculous.

But always: patience, practice, exploration and persistence.

They work.

STEP AWAY

Creative work is intense. You lose sense of time. Your mind is in another reality.

There is only so much of that anyone can take.

If you push too hard for too long, you -- and the work -- can get dull, muddy, reckless.

Now and then: stop. Do something else. Let your mind restore itself.

Everyone is different: some artists need to build up momentum, so the work they do after a couple of hours is the good stuff. Others start out hot and burn out fast.

Get to know yourself. There's no right or wrong way to do this, all that matters is how it works **for you.**

GET YOUR SCRIPT ON A SCREEN

Writing for screens shares elements with many other kinds of writing (playwriting, song lyrics, novels) and yet is stubbornly unique. It requires a set of obscure, complex skills.

That's why I suggest you try to record a couple of scenes.

I'm not talking about becoming a director or making indie movies. (I **am** a big fan of DIY and I urge you to look into that, but this is something else entirely.)

This is a private exercise. No one else needs to see it. It's just a way to help you understand what happens when a script is performed and recorded. Something about that process changes how your words work.

**nothing EVER comes out
like you imagine**

Choose A Simple Scene

A dialogue scene for just two or maybe three people. Nothing that requires a fancy location or physical action. If you don't have any such scenes: write a scene or two just for this purpose.

Give it an action: a beginning, middle and end. Set it in a location you can easily use: a living room or a kitchen. (Try to avoid exteriors, where sound becomes difficult.)

Write a good scene within those limits: something fun or scary or suspenseful or emotional.

Record The Scene

Get a couple of people to read it out loud, and make a video of it on your phone. That's the most crude version, but it will work.

If you happen to know actors -- great. If you want to try editing -- try it. But none of that is required.

Watch It -- Alone

It **will be garbage.** Be prepared for that. If you are the type of person who only sees the worst in what you do...still do this, but be aware: it requires you to see past the lack of acting ability and the crappiness of the visual experience.

The point is to get to some **basics**:

character

dramatic action

making dialogue work

Think of it like watching an elementary-school play: the basics of drama required to keep your interest and make action convincing are kind of brought forward when everything else is stripped-away (or done really badly).

What you're looking for are those magical moments in which your characters are truly talking to each other, trying to get something from the moment. That can happen even in the most horrible readings by the worst actors.

You don't need to do it often, but once or twice will be educational.

If you do this right, it's like unexpectedly catching a glimpse of yourself in a mirror -- not a lot of fun, but if you can get past the shock, it will tell you things you need to know.

It's a small, weird, awkward exercise, but what it helps with is crucial to writing for screens: making a moment happen -- creating dramatic energy between imaginary human beings.

GET A LIFE

Most creative people secretly believe their art is going to solve their personal problems. It won't.

If you put your life on hold for your work, or think your work will solve your life problems: when someone says, *"I don't love that first act transition,"* you feel as if they are threatening your life. You lash out or break down or run away.

It's just a note on a script.

Writing has to be a **part** of your life.

You may feel that you can't spend time on exercise or hobbies, clean your home, etc. until you've settled/fixed/ accomplished enough with your art. But there will always be creative problems, you are never "done" being an artist -- and having a miserable life puts extra pressure on your work.

If you're angry or frightened or desperate, you make bad artistic choices.

Figure out how to pay your bills. Take care of your health. Don't be an asshole. Find non-work-related things that you enjoy. Build a writing process you can do while you have a life and a job.

Many of the things that make people into artists are also emotional problems. Deep sensitivity, anxiety, hunger for connection, desire for control. Absolutely put them into your art -- but don't ask your art to solve them.

Everyone's version of this is going to be different. You know you. Just something to think about.

the art will thank you
by getting a whole lot better
when it doesn't have to
pay your rent &
fix your relationships

STORYTELLING
&
MECHANICS

6 ESSENTIAL QUESTIONS

As far as I can tell, these six questions are the basic stuff of storytelling:

who is it about?

what do they want?

why can't they get it?

what do they do about that?

why doesn't that work?

how does it end?

Let's look at them one by one:

Who Is It About?

A "character" is the messy complex sprawl of a human being, narrowed-down into a story. This is artificial, lives aren't stories -- but we instinctively try to put disorganized events into the form of an individual's experience. We look for a thread to follow.

So this sounds obvious, but you'll be amazed how often you lose track of it:

who are we following?
who do we care about?

(It doesn't have to be one, it can be two or more. Then you have to ask these questions about each, and figure out your priorities.)

What Do They Want?

If we know what somebody wants, we get involved. This is bizarre, but seems to be true.

We don't have to like them. They can want something we don't care about, or even something we think is stupid or evil -- but when we know they want something, we tend to think: *"I wonder if they're gonna get it?"*

In another words: *"What's going to happen?"* The magic mystery that makes us stay tuned and turn the page.

The audience rides on the tracks of this desire, this need.

Some call this the "objective," the "need" or the "goal." I prefer just calling it "what they want" -- because it's simpler, more human, less analytical.

Make The Thing They Want Specific

It can be an object (a box of money, or a bicycle) or an accomplishment (to publish a news story, get home, stay on their feet for fifteen rounds.) It can be an event or experience (their parent to show approval, their lover to accept a marriage proposal) or even information (to find out what happened to their sister.)

This narrow, concrete, specific thing they want often does represent or embody something larger and more general: love, or acceptance, or power -- but:

**keep what they want in the story SPECIFIC
so we can know when they GET it**

Tell Us What They Want

It's a good idea to state what they want, in dialogue, during the first third of the script. That's not an absolute rule, but it helps the audience know what to care about.

Luckily, if your character is going to take dramatic action -- change their situation, take risks, do difficult things -- they often want to tell someone about it.

What They Want Must Be Important -- Even If Only To Them

What they want can be obscure, small, even silly -- but the main character should want it a lot.

Otherwise when things get tough, why wouldn't they quit?

And things **should** get tough:

Why Can't They Get It?

A good name for this is "obstacles" -- and you need some, because:

Suppose your main character wants a glass of milk. They walk to the fridge and get it. They wanted something and took action and got it -- end of story.

Unfortunately, it's not much of a story.

But! If there is a lake full of piranhas between them and the refrigerator, now we've got a story. (Actually, a couple of stories -- since how this particular apartment came to exist would also be interesting.)

The Obstacles Have To Be Hard For The Main Character

It doesn't have to be life or death or saving the world. It doesn't even have to be universally recognized as hard. It just has to be hard **for them.**

For instance, if your main character wants a glass of milk but they have a terrible fear of refrigerators. Or if their family is pressuring them to lose weight, so the judgments and arguments they face getting that milk could be very painful.

Obstacles can be physical, social, psychological, or other characters.

The key thing is: they require the main character to take some kind of action.

What Do They Do About That?

Most of any story is made up of things the main character does to overcome obstacles and get what they want.

This is a basic engine of storytelling:

> **when a character has something they want,**
> **but it's not easy to get,**
> **they must take some kind of action**

These actions define the character. For example, if our character wants a glass of milk but there's a lake full of piranhas in the kitchen -- do they:

   try to float the sofa across to the fridge?

   or

   put together a team of ragtag quirky expert piranha hunters?

   or

   form a political party and try to change the building codes to end piranha lakes in kitchens?

Each of those choices suggest a very different person, with

different strengths, values and vulnerabilities.

Why Doesn't That Work?

During most of your story, what they do **doesn't work.**

(If they take action to get what they want and it works...your story is over.)

This is pretty logical: if the objective is important and the obstacles are substantial, it's gonna take a bunch of tries or steps to get it. In fact, a lot of the time what they do at first actually makes everything worse.

When what-they-do doesn't work -- they must adapt, adjust, learn things, find new or buried resources within themselves or face what they have to deal with in the world or in themselves.

So this sub-set of questions, repeated several times:

why can't they get it?

what do they do about that?

why doesn't that work?

-- makes up most of your story. Because until they've tried all the easy stuff and been pushed to learn or go to new places... they're not ready to do the thing they couldn't do.

That "thing they couldn't do" tends to be your ending.

How Does It End?

The ending centers on a final action that resolves the suspense at the heart of the story -- *is this person we have been following going to get what they want? What do they have to do to get it, or what decisively shows that they will not get it?*

Generally this climactic action is:

> different -- something they have never done before (otherwise, that earlier action would have ended the story)
>
> difficult -- otherwise why didn't they do it before?
>
> making use of skills, knowledge or things gained during the course of the story
>
> making some kind of statement on the larger emotions and ideas in the story's world or the hero's problems and desires

Failure is an option. Sometimes failing gives the character an education or revelation, sending them out of the story with a new sense of hope. But some stories are simply tragic (which, if you want a silver lining, is an education or revelation for the audience.)

The end of your story reflects back on everything that has happened. It sends the audience out with a feeling and a vision.

When you make the choice of how it will end, everything else gets easier to write. There are so **many** choices to make; the ending gives you a reason to make every other choice. The ending can save you, as a writer: go there early, plant your flag, set down your homing device.

Six questions.

They apply when working out a story, a character, a scene -- or even a bit of dialogue.

When you're stuck or lost or confused, when you don't know what to write or just don't feel like writing, these questions can help.

In 25 years as a professional screenwriter, I never found anything as versatile, reliable, reassuring or useful.

DRAMATIC ACTION

"Dramatic action" is not necessarily physical, and "dramatic" does not mean "big feelings." My definition of a dramatic action:

someone DOES something

But we don't sit down to watch people on a screen just buying their groceries or putting on their socks. So what's the difference between dramatic action and people just doing random stuff?

objective
&
change

Objective
is what the character is trying to accomplish, to get, to make happen.

(It can also be called a "goal", a "need" or an "intention." But I like to think of it as simply: what they want.)

at any given moment, each character
is trying to do something
to get what they want

that is their dramatic action

The "Super-Objective"
"What-they-want-**in-this-moment**" is almost always driven by a larger "what-they-want-**in-the-story**."

For example, in a particular scene: *they want to get a key away from another person.* But the reason they want the key is: *to open a box that has proof they are the rightful heir to the throne.*

So their objective in the scene is: **get the key.** Their storywide goal, their "super-objective" is: **take the throne.**

A character's dramatic action usually changes from scene to scene, in response to circumstances -- but this deeper thing they want should stay consistent all through the story.

In life we all have a jumble of shifting objectives, but in a story you choose one central thing-they-want and stick with it. That's one reason we like stories: they make more sense than life.

Change
When a character does something to get what they want, they are trying to make something change.

Even the most elaborate stunts or emotional outbursts are meaningless and ultimately boring if, after it happens, everything is the same.

This is why conflict is not necessarily action. If nothing changes, then conflict is just bad exposition presented via raised voices or clashing swords. Many actions that people take are not conflict: they apologize, cooperate, seduce, build, examine, inform, distract, exchange, etc.

Change can be a new direction, a step along a line of progress, getting a bit of information or even failure.

Internal changes can be dramatic action (for example, giving up on a plan) but there usually has to be some indicator we can witness: a declaration or conversation, a physical action.

So -- to get more specific about the definition:

**a dramatic action is
something a character DOES
in this moment
to get something they WANT
-- which results in a CHANGE**

Naming The Action

Looking for the dramatic action also leads to a valuable screenwriting tool -- an acting exercise every writer should know: for any scene, any moment, any character -- **choose a verb.**

Don't panic: "a verb" is just the **name** of an action. For example:

interrogate	build	distract
solve	demolish	attack
discover	soothe	praise
reveal	amuse	heal
convince	teach	accuse
deny	plant	step
reach out	reap	side
connect	confess	reassure
promise	bond	trick
trade	preach	confuse
create	test	sacrifice
decide	seduce	withdraw
analyze	reject	conceal
	feed	

When you choose one, you name the essential thing this character is doing at that moment. You focus on the scene's purpose and emotion. You give the actor something to do, which brings the moment to life. Choosing a verb is understanding dramatic action in its purest state.

For example:

> Murray drops a hint in a conversation with Brenda, to see if she knows about the upcoming party.

The verb then could be: **to test.**

But any action may have different verbs, depending on the story and context.

That's why verbs are so valuable: choosing a specific verb is about defining what you feel is **really** going on:

> Lois comes into the office, finds Jill and Joe. She asks Joe to get her a cup of coffee. When Joe does, Lois tells Jill something, privately.

The verb could be: **to exclude.**

But if what Lois was telling Jill might upset Joe -- the verb could actually be: **to protect.**

This is not a matter of getting it right or wrong. Different people will choose different verbs for the same scene or act. The point is making your choice and seeing each moment as action.

One note about verbs: a **few** *(be / are / is / was)* are passive. They describe "a state of being." **DON'T** use those when choosing "action verbs"! (It's okay -- but not great -- to use them when writing the text itself.)

Your character does not want to "be the queen" -- they want to **rule.**

They don't want to "be rich" -- they want to **make the sale** or **find the treasure.**

They definitely don't want to "be happy." Find another word: what action do they need to take to be happy?

As you work scene by scene, and especially when you're stuck or lost or just don't feel it -- ask yourself: **what is the action?**

THINK IN SCENES

Scripts are made out of scenes. The scene is the basic unit-- the building block -- of a script.

In fact, I think one of the best actual descriptions of what screenwriter does may be:

**screenwriting =
making everything into scenes**

When you're working alone and feeling lost, or when you're in a professional meeting and everyone is talking vague theoretical nonsense, you need to be thinking: *how am I going to turn this into scenes?*

Unfortunately, there is no universal formal definition of "a screenwriting scene." It is **not** defined in terms of shots or edits.

I believe the most useful way to define a scene is:

a scene is a DRAMATIC ACTION

Almost every scene I can think of is organized around a character doing something to try to get something they want.

While a scene often contains several actions, one will be most important: the "essential action," the organizing principle, what the scene is **about.**

For example:

```
A robot breaks through the wall of a
lab, killing a lab technician, then uses
unexpected-and-dazzling tech to defend itself
against attack by a security guard, and rolls
off down a highway.
```

The central action is: **the robot escapes.** It smashes and kills because it is escaping.

But: **the robot escapes** assumes it's a story about the robot. Suppose instead, the robot only violently escapes because it has been infected with malware by a villain -- and the "lab technician" is the true love of the hero, who will then be motivated to find and punish the villain.

Then the essential action of those exact same events is: **the villain kills the hero's true love.**

The action is the purpose and meaning of a scene. Finding it will steer how you write the scene.

So: if the robot-attack scene is about how **the villain kills the hero's true love**, you wouldn't bury the death of the lab technician/true love so early in the scene. You might show the robot defeating the guard first, and then have it kill the true love as the devastating climax to the scene. The fight with the guard is then only in the scene to establish the robot's intimidating power. The rolling-offdown- the-highway would be minimized, or even cut.

(Or, of course, maybe the guard IS the true love -- in which case the lab technician might be cut, or is just in the scene to prove the robot's recklessness or ruthlessness.)

This is not an analytic exercise. You're not done when you can say what the action is.

The central action is a **tool you use to write the scene.** It gives you a set of practical questions to ask:

what is the most consequential, emotional or revealing thing that happens in this scene?

who's taking that action?

what are they trying to do?

what are the obstacles they face?

For example: the character taking the action in the "robot attacks" scene is actually the off-screen villain. Does the villain **want** to kill the true love, or is the villain just trying to steal a robot, and the true love is collateral damage? Depending on that choice, you again might write the scene differently -- maybe going into the robot's POV, seeing it scan the faces of potential victims and reacting when it identifies its target, the true love.

I personally can't really write a scene without choosing the central action. Until I name it, I don't know what to focus on, how to describe what happens, where to steer the reader's attention and feelings.

A Scene Has A Shape: A Beginning And An End
And therefore you can ask:

> **what starts this scene?**
>
> what step, what plan, what thing they say?
>
> what triggers or motivates it?
>
> **what ends this scene?**
>
> do they get what they want, or do they fail?
>
> what is the consequence, the effect, of taking this action?

Ending the scene does not mean everything is resolved. In fact, almost always, even when it ends with a decisive action, a scene leaves a new or unresolved question.

Where In The Scene Does The Action Happen?
If it happens early, then the scene is about an action and its **consequences.**

If it happens at or near the end, it is about the events which **provoke** the action.

It can also take up the whole scene and be about the **process** of taking the action.

Script Format Helps You Define Scenes

One of the few good things about the clunky, restrictive format of scripts: a "Scene Heading" is about the **location** and **time** -- so:

**if you substantially change
TIME or PLACE
...it's probably a new scene**

Scene headings are easy to see, all-caps and double-spaced. Use them to remind yourself: *this is a scene! It starts, it ends, something is happening!*

How Long Should A Scene Be?

Scenes can be very short, sometimes just a few sentences --but most need half a page or more.

Industry wisdom says don't write scenes that run more than 3-or-4 pages.

But there are certainly examples of fantastic long scenes. These tend to be something of a set-piece: explore whatever makes it unique.

Watch a screen story you love, on a device you can pause, with a timeline Check how long various scenes are.

The standard calculation of screen time is: one page = one minute. Find a clock that indicates the passing seconds. Sit and watch it for a full minute. It's an agonizingly long amount of time.

**there are no absolute rules for
how long a scene should be
but usually, they need to move
faster than you expect**

The Undramatic Scene
It is possible to have a scene without a dramatic action.

Sometimes the filmmaker (or in a sense the film itself) is talking directly to the audience. For example: laying out a world before the action begins, or showing us a bomb hidden in a location the characters do not know about.

I would just advise: keep those short.

A Sequence = A Series Of Scenes Unified By An Action
Sometimes an action is big or complex, so it needs to be presented in a collection of scenes. They might even happen in different places and times but are all about one central action or idea.

For example:

at a party, we see several encounters between various characters

a heist, involving several distinct steps to pull off the theft

a chase, in which two characters are moving from one location to another

intercutting two scenes which relate to each other but take place with different people in different places.

a phone call, in which people in different places are in ascene together for the conversation

It's best to define the parts of these sequences with separate scene headings, since each part is also a unique scene.

Sequences tend to be set-pieces, high points, an important event or turning point in the story.

When you get lost or stuck, when it's all turning to crap...you need a clear, workable, specific task. The best one I know is:

think in scenes

SCRIPT FORMAT

Script format can be intimidating. But it's really just 6 basic elements, two of which you rarely use.

So it's not that hard -- but it **is** that important:

USE the standard format

If you don't, no one in The Industry will read your script.

Filmmaking is a complicated and demanding job, and professionals can't waste time on writers who don't respect its demands enough to learn the form. By using it, you indicate that you take the work seriously, and can operate within the system.

But nobody is measuring the number of spaces to your margins.

just get it to
LOOK LIKE A SCRIPT

(If you get lucky enough to have your script made, the producers will tell you the exact format they need.)

THE 6 BASIC FORMAT ELEMENTS

Scene Heading

Action

Character

Dialogue

Parenthetical

Transition

(NOTE: I'm using the names of these elements in Final Draft screenwriting software. More on software near the end of this chapter.)

I list the mechanical formatting details of each at the end of its section.

I'll use this script sample to break down the elements:

```
INT. MARY'S HOUSE - NIGHT

Jerry walks slowly through the silent rooms,
using his flashlight. He stops and sniffs the
air. Suddenly alert he turns, freezes.

He is scared out of his mind.

                    JERRY
          Is anybody here?

A big dog appears in the doorway.

                    JERRY
            (amused)
          Rufus.

Jerry kneels down and the dog lumbers over.
He pets it.

                              FADE OUT.
```

Scene Heading
(a.k.a "slug line")

The most distinctive and misunderstood part of a script. It has **only 3 parts:**

```
INT (or EXT). LOCATION - TIME
```

That's all: whether a scene is interior or exterior, and where and when it happens. So, in our example:

```
INT. MARY'S HOUSE - NIGHT
```

Sometimes, if a location has areas within it, you might add a second location:

```
INT. MARY'S HOUSE - BEDROOM - NIGHT
```

Keep your times very simple. Mostly stick to these four:

```
DAY

NIGHT

CONTINUOUS

THE SAME TIME
```

"Continuous" means the action continues directly from the scene before.

"The Same Time" is used if the scene is happening at (can you guess?) the same time as the scene before.

Use more detailed times only if it makes a difference in the story. If there's an actual ticking clock and the reader needs to know it's 4:17 pm, fine.

Likewise, if it matters in the story, you might use things like:

```
A HALF-HOUR LATER

SOON AFTER
```

But mostly, just stick to the main four.

If you're doing flashbacks, note it after the time:

```
INT. MARY'S HOUSE - NIGHT (FLASHBACK)
```

If it makes a difference in the story, or you have multiple different flashback times, note it in that parenthesis:

```
INT. MARY'S HOUSE - NIGHT (FLASHBACK - 1968)
```

Keep Scene Headings Consistent
Especially locations. Don't call it "THE STORE" in one scene and "THE SHOP" in another. This won't really matter until production, but it is subliminally confusing and annoying.

Don't Get Creative In Scene Headings
The most important thing to remember about Scene Headings: often people don't read them. Especially people who read a lot of scripts. So don't put any information in a Scene Heading beyond the location and time.

**ONLY use a scene heading to
CHANGE TIME or PLACE**

they are NOT for emphasis or to set a mood

"Scene Heading" Format
ALL CAPS
2 empty lines ABOVE it
1 empty line BELOW it
A period after "INT" or "EXT"
A DASH between the Location & Time

Some writers make the Scene Heading bold or underlined. I personally feel: why drag eyes toward the least dramatic part of script? It feels distracting.

Action
(a.k.a "Stage Directions" or "Body Text")

You use this for anything in a scene that isn't dialogue --
physical action, certainly, but also any kind of description,
narration, scene-setting, information or opinions:

```
Jerry walks slowly through the silent rooms,
using his flashlight. He stops and sniffs the
air. Suddenly alert he turns, freezes.

He is scared out of his mind.
```

write "action" in the present tense.

"Action Line" Format
Runs Width Of The Page
Single Spaced
Double Space Between Paragraphs

Character

A character's name, over any dialogue they speak.

```
JERRY
```

Keep Character Names Consistent
Don't call Mr. Jerry Jones "JERRY" in one scene and "MR.
JONES" in another.

Try Not To Have Character Names Look or Sound Alike
Unless that similarity is part of the story.

"Character Line" Format
All Capitals
Centered (over dialogue)
Double Space before

Single Spaced after
Next Line is "Dialogue"

Dialogue

This is for what a character says, when they speak in the script.

Is anybody here?

Do not use quotation marks around dialogue; the format tells the reader it is spoken, and the Character Name above tells them who is speaking.

"Dialogue" Format
Bigger margins, making a column in the center (i.e. indented approximately an extra inch from both the right and left margins of the "Action" line.)
No space between Character and Dialogue

That's basically it.

You can write an entire script using only those four elements: Scene Heading, Action, Character and Dialogue.

The other two elements are used only now and then:

Parenthetical

You use this to put a bit of description into the dialogue. It may tell us how the character says the line, or something the character does while saying it.

(amused)

Use these sparingly -- only for things the dialogue doesn't say. For example, you don't need:

```
                    VAL
      (adoringly)
   I love you, Basil!
```

You might need:

```
                    VAL
      (adoringly)
   Oh, Basil!
```

or

```
                    VAL
      (sarcastic)
   I love you, Basil!
```

Though I know excellent writers who disagree, I feel that parentheticals should be kept to one line.

<u>"Parenthetical" Format</u>
Indented 2-3 spaces from the left DialogueMargin
Single spaced to CHARACTER and DIALOGUE lines
Enclosed in parentheses

Transitions

This is used to note a screen technique for ending one scene and the transition into the next. For example:

```
                              FADE OUT.
```

Use these **very sparingly.** This is simply not a writer's job. It will be decided by the director and the editor, most likely in post-production.

I advise only noting a transition in the script if it makes a difference to the story. (Fading out usually indicates an ending for a section of the story, or a lingering finality to a moment. Dissolving indicates the passage of time, or a comparing/

contrasting of times, people or moods.)

I am also personally not a fan of "CUT TO." The "creative" use of "CUT TO" can be traced back to William Goldman's script for *Butch Cassidy & The Sundance Kid.* Because he did not know how to write a screenplay (he was a novelist at the time,) Goldman used it to suggest rhythm and emphasis. That script is truly a masterpiece, but the legacy of cut-to-ing is a problem.

The main reason: "CUT TO" uses up page space. You have so little space in a script! The basic way films get from one scene or shot to another is a cut: you don't have to say it.

"Transitions" Format
ALL CAPS
Justified to the right margin
Single Space below

At this point you have everything you need to format a script.

Final Draft offers another ten possible elements. I would suggest not worrying about them when you are learning to write a script.

("Act Breaks", for example, are only used if you are writing for television -- and even then, many series don't use them, and each company defines them differently.)

I urge you to focus on, and work within, the six basic elements. They're like the notes of a musical scale: few and simple, but if used well they can make any and every kind of music.

Some Other Format Notes

Use "Courier" Font

DO NOT Use Scene Numbers

Scene numbers are for, and applied by, the production. In a "reading script" they are distracting and annoying.

More's & Continued's

Again: a production will note when a scene continues on to another page -- but do **not** do this in a "reading script."

The only circumstance in which you should use "MORE" at the end of one page and "CONTINUED" at the top of another is if a dialogue speech is interrupted by a page break.

The Spaces-After-A-Period Controversy

To get nerdy on a topic that many people seem to get weirdly heated over: should there be two spaces after a period?

Computers automatically adjust the space after a period. Typewriters did not. Script software, however, uses the "Courier" font, which tries to reproduce typewriting and therefore does **not** create additional space between sentences.

I think it is good to have a bit of space after a period. It helps separate thoughts and lets you play with rhythm. It keeps your type from becoming an intimidating block. If your software is not adjusting the space automatically, I suggest adding the extra space.

Software

You DO NOT NEED SPECIAL SOFTWARE TO WRITE A SCRIPT.

It certainly can make it easier - but The basic elements can be formatted as "styles" in most word-processing programs.

The advantage to using script-writing software is you can type scripts faster. Many can do nifty things like outline mode, note cards, etc.

But until you get comfortable with it, the software may actually slow you down and confuse you. And software is expensive.

If you have the money, the time to get familiar, and plan on writing many scripts -- sure, get scriptwriting software.

I personally like and use Final Draft. It's excellent, and gets better all the time. Most people in The Industry also seem to use it. (When not writing scripts, and for script outlines, I use Scrivener, which is great but takes some getting used to.)

There is free script software out there, which I have not tried. I would advise not working on any software that only lets you store your work on their servers. Keep your scripts, they are your property.

I also urge you not to use writing software that prompts you with creative ideas or suggestions.

The Most Important Thing To Remember About Script Format

Screenwriters use the format because they have to, but it does also have a sweet side-effect -- it requires you to see everything as:

broken into SCENES (Scene Heading)
people SAYING stuff (Character & Dialogue)
people DOING stuff (Action)
&
what we SEE & HEAR (Action)

Script format helps you shape your story into scenes, and emphasizes dramatic action.

format is A WAY OF THINKING

HOW TO ORGANIZE A PROJECT

Creative writing is hard. Setting up a consistent process means you don't have to think, *"how do I write?"* every time you get to work -- you just think about the thing you are writing.

**the work happens more easily
when it has a place to go**

Your work-organizing method should be:

affordable

something you can get to and use easily

something you own and control

This is a system I worked out for myself, over time. It's pretty basic, so it works with different technologies and types of project. For me, creating and using these documents/folders serves as a method, a routine, a ritual.

I create a **folder** with five **documents** in it:

Overview

Notes

Outline

Text

Research

Let's look at what's in each:

Overview

This is where I write down organizational and theoretical stuff.

statements of plan or purpose

character lists, sketches, analysis

themes & ideas

references & models to look at

genre notes

the major moves

instructions to myself (like "make it funny")

It's for anything that isn't in the work itself -- stuff I want to think about or remember that doesn't belong in the outline or the text.

Notes

This is where I talk to myself, on paper. It's an endless scroll scratchpad, a daily whiteboard.

Each work day I add a "date line" and then get to it. Whatever's on my mind, whatever the task is.

I write notes to myself, remind myself of problems and goals, stages of the work. I ask and answer questions. I try things out. I argue with myself, complain, puzzle. Anything goes.

Most of it will never be looked-at again, and that's fine.

When I write something I like, something concrete and specific -- I copy that bit into the appropriate other documents, mostly the Outline and Overview.

Outline

This is a list of scenes -- a place to note, sketch, describe and organize everything I can think of that may go into the story.

I use a home-made outline format, which I lay out in detail in the chapters "Why Outline" and "How To Outline."

Text

This starts out as a place to put scraps of text, if I think of any. Eventually it will be the entire manuscript itself.

As it grows bigger, the Outline gets smaller: as I write details and ideas as text, I delete them from the Outline, so it starts to work as a "things to do list."

If stuff remains in the Outline, unused in the text -- then the Outline serves as a place to think about what these are and why they're not quite working.

Ideally, when the rough draft of the text is done, the Outline is just a string of mostly-empty index cards, a list of scenes. Then the Outline is ready to be used as a work space for new notes and questions, per scene, for the rewrite.

Research

A place where I can collect bits of fact, background and inspiration.

A lot of it is typed-out or copied-and-pasted from other sources.

I put it in a distinctive font or color, to make sure I never accidentally use it directly in the text.

Down the line, a project may include a few other folders:

Research Materials
For PDFs of whole articles, pictures, maps and whatever.

Archive Folder

Every so often I'll save a copy of the outline or the text, date it, and keep it in this. floder Especially if I'm at a turning point (like starting a new draft) or if I substantially rethink something and want to keep a version with the original idea intact. Just in case. You never know.

Biz/Legal

A place to keep notes from calls, correspondence, memos or contracts, lists of people it was submitted to, etc.

So there it is: a work place, a work plan.

Pretty much anything I can do for a project will belong in one of these documents.

Each project is different and requires variations -- but for me, it helps to have a place for each "type of thinking."

As I work, I start out mostly in the Overview and Notes, but over time I am opening the Outline first every day...and then after a while I'm in the Text most of the time.

Try it out. See if it works for you. Everyone works in a different way. Figure out yours, by trying things.

How will you know if it works for you? You'll get stuff done. You'll be thinking about the work itself, not the process.

WHY OUTLINE

An outline is a list of scenes. It's a place to work in.

You do not have to outline. If you're writing scripts and it's going well and they come out like you want -- keep doing what you're doing.

But if you're stuck, lost or scared...an outline is a possible process to get you past those problems.

The Outline Is A Way To Think

It organizes your thoughts into scenes. It steers you to prioritize and start making choices. It helps you look at cause and effect, setup and payoff. It shows you what you've got and what you need.

Making An Outline Is A Creative Act

You don't need to "save" your inspiration for the text itself. You don't "use up" creativity. The outline simply adds another, different place in which to play.

You discover, improvise and invent **while** you outline. You'll be surprised how much emotion one can get out of outlining.

The outline helps focus your creativity by making the work specific, putting things into scenes. (Being specific matters. If I say: "be creative!" most people freeze up. But if I say: "write a scene where a character has to get an ankle bracelet off another character who is sleeping" -- you start to work.)

Action, description and dialogue will pop into your head when you're figuring out what scene goes where -- write them down! Put them in the outline! You can move them into the text down the line.

And later, when writing the script, there will still be more than enough you need to discover and invent.

An Outline Does NOT Set Everything In Stone.
An outline is just a plan. It's a tool -- a way look at the story, a place to think and try things out. You don't have to make it perfect, or even stick to it.

You can change the outline as you write, and between drafts.

It is a working tool, to which you keep going back during the entire process.

The Outline Remembers
Most people can't hold every step of a story in their head.

It Makes You More Flexible
It's easier to change the outline than rewrite whole scenes.

You Step Back
It is very hard to see the structure while working on the text. Looking at a list of scenes helps you catch repetition and tangents, feel pace and rhythm. You can see if something is missing in the story. It is a way of getting to know your story, themes and characters.

It Helps You Know When You're Ready To Write
If you use an outline format with a distinctive style for questions (like the one I lay out in the chapter "How To Outline"), you can skim through and get an immediate sense of where you're not yet sure of what a scene or character is about.

When you get down to just a few unanswered questions, you feel more confident that it's time to plunge into the world of the text.

It Minimizes Waste, Frustration And Loss

Following impulse and feeling can take you to fascinating and beautiful places, but you can also paint yourself into a corner or write good things that have no place in the story.

It feels crappy to write something good and then have to throw it away. Thinking through the big picture in the outline reduces the number of frustrating and painful dead ends.

It Helps When You're Stuck

Writing a narrative is a journey. You will always blunder and explore. But the process can get disheartening if you **just** blunder and explore.

The outline truly does help, letting you work and think in a simplified version.

Professional Collaboration

An outline is often a required step in professional writing work. "Breaking a story" is the television-room phrase for writing a detailed outline.

If you are hoping to work in The Industry, get comfortable with this way of working.

Outlining is an artificial process, stepping away from the audience experience and going behind the scenes, into the mechanics behind the magic.

It takes practice to get used to it.

But once you do, it brings its own joys: new ways of problem-solving, mastery of the craft, a more flexible process to face the endless puzzles, doubts and fears that stop us from writing.

HOW TO OUTLINE

There is no right or wrong way to make an outline.

Only you can figure out how your particular brain works -- not how it ought to work, or how someone says it works, or how any other brain works.

Use the technology and format that works for you: paper index cards, a three-ring binder, flow-chart software or a word-processing document.

Try things out. Pay attention to how it goes. See what actually works.

(To help with that: at the end of this chapter I've written a list of questions to ask yourself while trying out different ways to outline.)

Below is the method I've worked out for myself over the years. Try it out and see if it works for you.

My Outline Format

This approach breaks down to 4 basic elements:

```
Scene Line
Details
Questions
Notes
```

I set them up as "Styles," which should work in almost any type of word processing software. Or, in the physical world, you could use colored pens, or just underline and indent stuff.

I use different colors for each style, for a visual sense of what I've got and what I need to get. Since this book is only in black-

and-white, I've just tried to make them distinctive by using font and size.

Here is a sample:

Amy Tells Him His REAL Job

He might protest. She says you want the job or not?
Arlo: what the hell. What am I looking for?
I don't know. Just look. Listen. Find out what they're saying. These people destroyed my father. They're evil. I just want to know what they're doing. Go tell me what they're doing.

> *suspense right away: he has an UNCOMFORTABLE mission*

Arlo Goes To Spy - Finds Bloggers

He takes trash bags, to pretend to be cleaning

Are they SNEAKING IN?

Spying Begins - Bond With Venice

Goes to spy, they're friendly and interesting.
Venice off by himself

What is Venice's attitude at this point?
Lulu doesn't want to talk much.
Joblin Buys Arlo Lunch

Venice Badmouths Kornish & Amy To Arlo

Confides in him...bonding
Kornish's history (Someone looks at the list of clients)

Do we find this all out now - or just hint at it?
I think just hint

> *We believe Kornish is the villain at this point*

Amy Mourning Rituals

The Scene Line

An outline is a list of scenes. This style is a scene's **name**: its headline, its title. This line is a way to capture the **heart** of the scene: the action, the center, the purpose.

(It is **not** a script format "Scene Heading" -- it's not about interiors, exteriors, location, etc.)

I keep these short -- ideally one line.

Sometimes I already know the emotional heart or use of the scene, so simply identifying it is all I need - like:

> **Joe And Sue Drive In The Desert**
>
> **Jerry In The Diner With Ruth (Jerry's Monologue)**

But it could also name the dramatic action :

> **Joe Confronts Sue About The Dog**
>
> **Joe and Sue Bond A Bit While Driving**

The point is to get myself to see each scene as an action, a step in the story -- to remember that despite the many things that may happen in it, there's one central reason this scene exists.

"Scene Line" Format
I format it larger (14 point) and bold, with some space around it (at least 2 empty lines above) so it feels more weighty and structural than everything else on the page.

The Details Line

This style is for **anything** that might go in the scene.

It can be just a couple of stray notes, or a 2-page long beat by-beat description of what happens. It could include bits of dialogue, descriptions of the costumes or settings, analysis of the characters.

I brainstorm here, this is a work space. I throw stuff in, take it out. It's a place to collect all the rough possibilities and slowly refine them over time.

Joey Has A Breakdown

```
Joey empties the refrigerator.  As he does,
he talks on speakerphone to the parole office
-- lying about everything.

Does he care what happens to the stuff he's
taking out?

He drinks a beer while he talks.
```

```
            "Details Line" Format
         I format this very simply.
You're going to be seeing a lot of this style,
        so make it comfortable to read.
     Think of it as your basic "body text."
```

Those two styles are really the bottom line, the bare-bones essential. If all you had was **scene lines** and **details** -- you could outline a whole script.

But I like to set a couple of **types of detail** apart:

The Questions Line

A way of reminding myself: *you still have to figure this out.*

Joey Has A Breakdown

```
Joey empties the refrigerator.  As he does,
```

117

```
he talks on speakerphone to the parole office
-- lying about everything.

Does he care what happens to the stuff he's
taking out?

He drinks a beer while he talks.
```

Sometimes I use these to lay out alternatives, a choice yet to be made.

Ideally, they're one way to know I'm ready to write: when I don't have any of this style left in my outline. But in truth, some things stay questions that can't be answered until I write the scenes.

"Questions Line" Format
This is essentially a "details line" but with something to make this style stand out, so you can see there's something you need to resolve.
(In this book I have made it italic-and-underlined, but when I have color to work with, I make these bright pink.)

The Notes Line

This style is for when I have something to say about the scene but it doesn't go in the scene: theory, reminders, notes-to-self, summary, character thoughts.

Keep this short!
DAY 3 of their vacation.
This is where he reveals his true evil nature.

"Notes Line" Format
I want to remember these bits

```
        are not going in the script,
            so I center them.
```
(In this book I have made them italic-and-bold,
but when I have color to work with,
I make these blue or purple.)

I think these four styles cover everything you need to outline pretty much any kind of script.

But you think of something else you need, do it!

I add styles for particular projects -- like "Act Break" for TV, or "chronology" for a story that moves between time periods, or "Possible Event" (like "Scene Line" in a different color) when brainstorming scene ideas.

You know you. Make it work.

A Nifty Outline Trick: The Scene List

I turn the outline into a checklist to track where I am as I write a draft.

FIRST make a COPY of the outline!
DO NOT use your outline!
MAKE A COPY!

Delete everything except the scene lines.

Reformat so it fits on one page. It doesn't matter how small the type is.

Then as I write a draft -- I cross each scene off when I've done it.

Outline Software

You do not need special software to make an outline.

There's a lot of cool software out there -- but only use it if you can afford it **and** it helps you. (See questions on helpfulness, below.)

I strongly urge you not to use any software that tells you how to write your story. Some software sets out "required" plot points, character types, etc. If you want to use a formula or system from a book or a class and it's working -- go for it. But don't have it baked into your software.

Questions To Ask About Your Outline System
A list of questions to ask yourself when trying to decide if an outline system is working for you:

is it turning everything into scenes?

is it showing you what the action is and who's taking it?

does it allow physical space for all your thoughts?

does it give you ways to distinguish questions, problems or thoughts from events in the story?

does it help you organize and prioritize?

does it help you explore and experiment?

does it allow you to step back and look at the story or structure?

is it easy to make changes, rethink, reorganize?

is it showing you what's ready-to-write and what's not?

is it safe? can you lose it? can you back it up?

is it easy for you to operate?

can you afford it?

are you thinking more about content than process/ technology?

do you find yourself looking forward to using it?

an outline is a TOOL

**it's a place to work in
a way to gather your materials,
organize and refine them,
a way to build a list of scenes**

No one else is looking at it. All that matters: make it work for you.

CHARACTER

You may be devoted to dazzling action, hilarious jokes, complex world-building, twisty plots or important ideas -- but for an audience, those things only exist in terms of characters.

Human beings understand everything in terms of human beings. A movie about rats or talking micro-organisms is still about people.

But more than that:

characters FEEL
characters CHOOSE
characters ACT

And that is the stuff of stories. Characters are the cause, the engine, the basis of stories.

Let's start with a cliche and try to make it useful:

character is action

We understand people -- they reveal themselves -- through what they do. If you want a character to be something, they have to **do** things to make that true.

This gives you a useful writing trick:

if you are jammed-up on your STORY --
think about it in terms of CHARACTER

If you don't know what happens next, think about who is involved: What are they like? What do we know about them? What do they want?

...and at the same time:

if a CHARACTER is not working --
think about their actions in the STORY

If you don't feel like a character is right or strong enough -- think about what they **do.** What does that tell you about them?

So: character is action...except that would mean they would just do the same thing, over and over. Clearly, "character is action" is not enough.

characters
UNFOLD
DEVELOP
PLAY OUT

A character is defined by what they do -- but they do more than one thing. A story is a whole series of actions, in which any one is just a piece of the big picture. Therefore:

character is a SEQUENCE of actions

For example:

```
"A" puts their cigarette out in "B"'s eye.
```

That's a pretty vivid, memorable character-defining action, right? So now we **know** "A" is a vicious, sadistic, evil person. Except then:

```
"A" puts out their cigarette in "B"'s eye
-- then goes to church to pray.
```

Now: is "A" a hypocrite? Or is "A" a truly religious person who has a problem with impulse control and feels guilty about what they did? Or is "A" someone with short-term memory loss?

What if:

> We meet "A" working in a microbiology lab, hunting a deadly new virus...and right before the cigarette incident we see the virus get into lab-assistant "B"'s eye. If it is not burned-out in the next four seconds, it will spread and kill everyone in the world!

actions only have MEANING
in the CONTEXT of other scenes

This stuff is insanely important, so I'm going to repeat it:

character is a SEQUENCE of actions

characters
UNFOLD
DEVELOP
PLAY OUT

actions only have MEANING
in the CONTEXT of other scenes

But just because they're going to unfold or develop does not mean you start characters out as boring. You **start** them as interesting, and then make them **more** interesting.

when we meet a character,
they should be DISTINCTIVE,
but NOT COMPLETE

Establish characters simply, with some strong, clear emotion or idea or story, and then let them develop complexity as they go.

a character can develop in two essential ways:
they can CHANGE
or
we can REVEAL deeper layers

They're both good, and you can do both in the same story or even the same character. They are just **mechanisms** by which we understand characters more deeply as a story goes on. Put them in your toolbox and ask: *am I doing at least **one** of these with this character?*

The secret key to character:

What do any of us really know about other people? Only what we can figure out from what they **do** and **say**.

So the audience comes into the story ready to "read" your characters as they do real people. Don't put everything on the surface, don't explain everything. Let it build, let it develop -- let the audience work on the characters, uncover them, figure them out.

Your job is to think of your characters as human beings even in ridiculously made-up situations. Don't make everything easy. Give them room to be messy and emotional and human.

Care about people -- and your stories will work.

CREATING A CHARACTER

Character Biographies
Thinking through the story of a character's offscreen life, choosing their favorite songs and what their parents did for a living, can provide texture and depth for their actions and dialogue.

But it can also distract or mislead you.

You can start to feel like this character is interesting because of all the stuff you know about them that isn't in the script.

It's important to think of the character biography as a tool, like improvisation: a way to stir up your creativity about the script, but not an end in itself.

Character Description
Try to avoid physical description. If you were an actor, would you rather be in a scene where you're trying to be blond with high cheekbones -- or where you have a specific emotional action to play?

If their physical body or the way they dress is important to the action -- then sure, describe it. But otherwise, describe characters in terms of:

  behavior

  attitudes

  beliefs

  mannerisms

  style

  emotions

Characters Exist In Relationships

They may be a "hero" or a "villain" but in the story, and in their world, they are also a boss, an employee, a friend, an enemy, a parent, a servant, a teacher, a lover. Even "a loner" is involved in the relationship of keeping people at a distance (or being excluded.)

This means you need to look at character not just in terms of the story you want to tell, but also how each character relates to the others.

Writing A Character For A Specific Actor

Generally: don't do it.

It can be inspiring to imagine a particular actor in a role, but don't try to identify or name them in the script. For one thing, you often end up trying to reproduce a specific performance. Good actors don't usually like to play the same character over and over. They want distinct playable action, strong unique characters.

And when that imagined actor doesn't take the role, you have to substantially rewrite it.

If you **are** inspired by a specific actor, think about the defining characteristics that person brings. Tap into the archetype -- but then use that to create a new, unique character who can live in your story.

Character Research

If this character has a job or lives in a place: learn about it. Explore it. What's it like to be that person?

What's possible for this person? Use the world: the news and the internet are feeding you characters all day, every day. Get in the habit of keeping a "scrap pile" of articles, images and even videos that capture human beings, because human beings are really various and interesting.

Use people you know, their mannerisms or personalities or quirks (but transformed, changed, reimagined!).

Use stuff from your life. Follow your feelings and impulses. If you like some kind of food or music or know about something -- give that to a character.

Whatever you bring to your characters is what makes them feel alive, because life is unpredictable, created by a billion personal experiences.

CHARACTER "DEPTH"

You hear a lot about characters being "shallow" or "flat," which is clearly bad -- but what does that mean in a practical sense? Here's how I look at it:

character "depth" comes from
being defined by
more than one thing

A nerd who sabotages is different from a nerd who rescues. A lawyer who steals may be a thief, or -- if they steal to buy their child vital medicine -- a parent.

No human being is or does only one thing. They have jobs, hobbies, beliefs, passions, communities, friendships, families, physical and psychological conditions. The more of these things a character has going on, the "deeper" they will be.

The name "depth" is not really accurate. It's more like "character complexity."

Real people are incredibly complex. They are essentially incomprehensible.

But a screen story only has so much time and space. Too much character complexity makes the story slow or confusing.

One reason we like stories is that they prioritize life's insane layers of character -- which is a lie about life, but one we seem to need.

writing a story means choosing
to make one part of a person
most important and meaningful

While you can never "solve" the balance of simplified storytelling artifice versus the impossibly nuanced reality of human beings...trying to do both is central to the art.

MINOR CHARACTERS

We often create characters to perform a task in the central character's story:

inform or advise

motivate

interact to support

interact as obstacle

mirror with contrast or variation

But your need to have them serve this function is **not** a motivation for **them.**

minor characters don't KNOW they're minor characters

Every one of them is the central character in their own movie. They enter and leave each scene with their own objective.

Take the time to think out each of your characters' stories. (You can use the techniques described in the chapter "Building Character Arcs.") It makes a difference.

In some ways a minor character's arc needs to be **more** clear and intense, since we have fewer scenes in which to understand them.

Keep it simple. Most supporting characters will only have one or two defining characteristics, beyond their plot function. They're rude, romantic, sarcastic, scared, scary.

But give them a little bit of growth or change, or reveal a little bit of unexpected complexity. A little "depth" goes a long way.

BUILDING CHARACTER ARCS

Every character, even the most insignificant supporting bit, thinks everything is happening in **their** movie. They're living their own full life -- but we're only seeing a few slices of it.

You need to make sure those slices come together to make a line.

That's the "arc" of the character.

This gives you a simple, brilliant way to write better characters:

Go through the script looking at it only through one character's eyes. Think about them as the main character of **their** story.

Let's say a supporting character shows up during three scenes in your story. If you only think of those moments as separate beats, providing whatever's fun or useful in regard to the main character -- the audience feels a hidden shallowness or falseness.

But if we give this minor character their own (mostly invisible) story, not only does it help you write their scenes -- it helps the main story feel more real, more alive.

Here's how to do it:

Make An Outline For Each Character
Make a copy of your outline and cut out any scene the character is not in. This might leave half the script, or only two scenes.

Now look at their scenes. Ask:

> what does the story require them to do?

> what do those actions tell you about this person?

Brainstorm what kind of person would do that stuff, and why:

> considering what we know they **do** -- who are they?
>
> what is their attitude towards the things the story has them doing?
>
> what do **they** think each scene is about?
>
> what are they trying to do in the story, and in each scene?
>
> is this person consistent, wanting the same thing in all of their scenes?
>
> how and why do they change as the story goes on?

Try To Give Each Character A "Moment"

Some useful action or emotional beat. Let them be unexpectedly helpful or brave or disappointing or funny. Find their feeling, their style. There's always **something** you can give them.

Give Them Something To Say

Supporting characters can give us variations and alternative views on the themes or problems of the main story. They can disagree with the main character, or inform them. You can make an observation or state an opinion through them, or about them.

Give Them A Bit Of Progress

Try to give them some kind of change from scene to scene, even if it's just doing more of whatever they are. Reveal them, or let them show their value to the story, in steps.

By making a character outline, instead of writing a character biography, you're only allowing yourself to work with the materials that will be seen by the audience. Don't give a two-scene character an elaborate backstory -- just make them interesting while we're watching them.

Actors and directors will love you for doing this. If you don't think a character through, then they have to do that for you.

This understanding of character is especially useful when writing a series, because at some point the show may explore some minor character in depth, even if only for an episode.

This method is simple -- but remarkably powerful. The reader doesn't even know why, but they get more engaged when you take a minute to give each character their own life.

CHARACTERS AND CHANGE

Does Your Main Character Have To Change?
No...but **something** does.

Maybe your unchanging character changes someone else. Or your character is trying to stay who they are in a world that is changing. Or they have moved to a new world.

The task then is to steer audience expectations to the story you're telling.

Make us want the character to stay the same. Make their unchanging characteristics admirable, or create a painful consequence if they give them up. Or tell a tragic tale about the character's doomed conflict with time or place or others.

Make sure the audience knows what to **want** and what to **fear** for the unchanging character.

Unchanging Doesn't Mean Easy
A character who doesn't change cannot just move through the story doing the same thing over and over. Even if they won't change, the story still has to push them to adjust their plans or actions as they face obstacles.

Another answer to this problem (the answer to most things) is depth. Complexity. They may be unchanging -- even super-powered -- in one way, but vulnerable in others.

Does A Main Character Need To Learn Something?
The main character is going to face a difficult obstacle, which means almost always they **do** have to learn something, see something in a new way, or find something in themselves to cope with it.

That said, some stories just raise questions. Some present us with characters who hold opposing beliefs, both (or all) of which have some value. Sometimes the main character teaches another character something. Or the audience will learn something by watching a character fail to learn it.

So while a character often will have to learn, what they learn is not necessarily something the audience is supposed to take away for themselves. It **can** be -- but a script is certainly not required to include a spoken "lesson."

ATTRIBUTES, TYPES & ARCHETYPES

Attributes

Many teachers, books and software suggest you develop characters by making charts or lists of qualities, traits, characteristics. I'm not a fan.

Characters do have "strengths & weaknesses" or "wounds & dreams" or "inner needs & outer needs"...but these attributes need to be revealed or played out in dramatic actions with other characters or they don't exist.

Further: attributes interact. Most of us have conflicts between parts of ourselves. They are not set and static. A character is often defined by the evolving relationships, the struggle, between different needs or feelings.

If you want to give a character an attribute, work on where it will play out in action, dialogue, scenes.

Types

A "type" is a character who has been reduced to a single attribute. Physical description, social class or clique, a job or interest, coming from a specific place or culture -- these are all legitimate **elements** of a character. But they cannot, by themselves, **define** a character.

The problem with types is they become stereotypes: they assume a physical quality, job or social status means we know that person's feelings or experience.

If you assume that: you're not just a bad writer, you're kind of a bad person.

But our concern here is that stereotypes are static and dull.

Giving characters "strong" types" doesn't make them any less types. Professions like "sex worker" or "professional killer"

136

appear to make the characters "dramatic," since they require vivid actions during their working day -- but a vivid action without a goal and an obstacle is just meaningless stimulus, a poke to which we will soon become numb.

Types **can be** useful. They provide a set of expectations. You can use these to subvert and surprise, by giving a "type" unexpected actions that reveal and define them not only as players in a drama, but as humans who provoke thought and feeling.

In other words: every character deserves a bit of "depth." **If** at all possible, define them by more than one thing, give them more than one thing to do.

Archetypes

I also want to make a distinction between Stereotypes and Archetypes.

"Archetype" is a complex concept with different meanings in psychology, philosophy and literary theory -- which you should look into.

In terms of creative writing, I look at archetypes this way: if you want to use mythic or psychological categories as the beginning of a character -- swell! A character **may be** a Bully or a sSeducer or a King Lear or a Penelope...but they still have to be a character in **your story**. You still have to give them a unique set of dramatic actions, relationships and some "depth."

CHARACTER FLAWS AND "LIKEABILITY"

Complexity means: not all parts of your character will be good. And that's okay! A flawless character doesn't match our experience of human beings.

But character flaws can make us dislike a character.

Here are some ways to give a character flaws without making them a hateful person:

Think Of The Flaw As An Obstacle In The Story
Show us the flaws as something we fear will undermine their ability to get what they want. Then they struggle with it, too.

Recognize That Most Flaws Are Also Virtues
"Recklessness" can part of be "Bravery," "Arrogance" can be too much "Confidence," "Obsession" can be "Passion" taken too far.

Use The Flaw To Explore Insight And Empathy
Most flaws come from emotions we may recognize in ourselves. Be thoughtful and truthful about where they come from, about why we feel them or how conflicted we are about them.

It's easy to judge characters harshly or think of them as just parts of your plot, but the actual name for thinking that way is "contempt" and it's corrosive. Your story may eventually condemn them -- but as you write them, moment to moment, you really can't.

do not LOOK DOWN on your characters

Let them be who they are. Don't try to make everything nice. Don't hold back. If they are pedantic, or dumb, or irritable...let them be. Use it, dramatically. If they only have one moment of kindness: fine. If they have none, how does that play out in the story?

Figure out who they are and don't apologize. Don't write defensively.

"Likeability"

There is often great concern in The Industry that characters be "likable."

We **do** want to feel drawn to, and empathize with, our central character. But the hunger for "likeability" often becomes a need to make them ideal, or to imitate the popular. The desire to make characters "relatable" can steer us toward cliches.

I think this betrays a serious misunderstanding of how stories work. Audiences often use characters to explore emotions or actions that we would never want to act out in reality. Characters endure terrible things, make stupid mistakes, learn painful lessons, so we don't have to.

Admiration and aspiration are not the only ways we care about a character. Stories can show us we have things in common with people we despise, or pity, or who seem very different.

Audiences have taken so many foolish, wrong-headed, even monstrous characters to their hearts that, as far as I can tell:

**we can care about ANY character
as long as they WANT something
but face an OBSTACLE
and TAKE ACTIONS to get what they want**

This is just my personal theory, but this is my personal book.

MULTIPLE CENTRAL CHARACTERS

Can you have more than one central character? Absolutely.

A "Two Hander"

is what The Industry calls a story about a relationship: romances or romantic comedies, "buddy stories," many "road movies."

In these, both main characters are equally important and the story has to resolve both personal arcs.

Ensembles

tell stories of multiple central characters -- sometimes in a group that interact, or sometimes interweaving separate lives who may or may not meet but explore variations on a theme.

In some ensembles the "world" or the "moment" are the center, and the characters are aspects of that complex topic. For example, *Nashville* (1975), *Treme* (2010-2013), or *Do The Right Thing* (1989).

But even within ensembles there is often a central person, in terms of:

> how much time we spend with them
>
> how central their actions are to the story
>
> who ends the story

And since the last action or moment often defines a story, and the characters can't **all** have that moment -- you either need to devise an action or event that resolves multiple stories, or you need a series of smaller endings in which one actually comes last.

The other challenge with multiple main characters: each

character takes screen time from the others, and having too many can get confusing or overwhelming.

Juggling storylines is an art, and a skill. If you want to do it, study work that does it. And, as with any skill, you master it through practice and the experience of trial and error.

It's certainly more complicated to tell a story with multiple main characters -- but the satisfaction and power when you pull it off can be more intense than a simple story.

The point: it's possible, and a good writer should keep possibilities in their toolbox.

DIALOGUE

The emotional and narrative power of dialogue cannot be overstated. Think about your life, your relationships, how you get things done. Now try to take the talking out of that.

If you want to write a script about human beings and their lives, they almost always need to talk to each other.

The ability to write dialogue is a gift. Shifting into different voices comes easier to some writers than others. But even if it doesn't come easily, you can learn the mechanics and -- with practice -- develop the skill.

The most important thing to remember:

dialogue is action

Stop thinking about dialogue as a way to convey information.

You can't make the audience believe or feel something by just stating it. Even a character saying, "I love you," or "I hate you," will carry little emotional weight if it doesn't have an effect on the characters in the moment.

If you want a character to convey information, they need a convincing personal reason in that moment to do so.

Think about what each character is trying to accomplish when they speak. Are they trying to:

comfort	evade	give an order
impress	seduce	make a choice
intimidate	lie	announce news
interrogate	manipulate	(and so many more...)
confess	convince	

The inescapable next question is then:

What Is The EFFECT Of A Line?

Did it accomplish what the speaker intended? What action does that provoke in the person they are talking with? If it didn't work as intended: what does the character do about that? Do they move on? Try again with more force? Break down, give up? Change their approach? To what?

Dialogue is all "dramatic actions" and "adjustments" (see the chapters on each of these topics.) It's often like the characters are playing a game: each player is making their move when they speak.

Some Nifty Dialogue Hacks

Read It Out Loud

Does it sound like someone talking? Are the sentences so long you lose the point or need to take a breath? Are there words or sounds that are hard to say next to each other?

Writing for screens requires unnatural compression. A lot of the art of dialogue is creating the illusion of living speech in a highly-artificial form.

End The Conversation

Have something change, raise a new question, have it be interrupted or even clearly left hanging. Just let us know this particular interaction is done.

Use An Action Line To Break Up Dialogue For Rhythm Or Emotion

```
                    SAM
          Stop.  I don't want to hear
          any more lies. I trusted
          you.

He turns away, so Jeff won't see his tears.

                    SAM
          You were my friend.
```

Don't do this too often, as it hinders the pace -- but in a key moment, when you want to slow it down, this can make a line hit harder.

It can also be helpful when you want dialogue to be indirect or subtext-y but you fear (or find) that readers don't get the point. Instead of making the line explain everything, add a bit of insight for the actors and director (and reader):

```
                    JOYCE
          I was thinking maybe you
          should pick up the flowers.


She smiles tightly.  Trying hard not to say
she wants a divorce.

                    JOYCE
          Or maybe not.
```

Ask Yourself: Does It Flow?
Does each line somehow come from the last line and lead to the next? Even an interruption, tangent or change of subject

can be a part of the flow of a scene.

Look out for lines that just stand there alone, unprompted and with no consequence, or lines that stop a flow dead.

Ask Yourself: Is It "News"?
Try not to show us people telling each other stuff they already know -- or that we already know.

If you want us to see a character's reaction to something we already know, try to come into the scene after they hear the recap -- or make the way they are told original and interesting, make it an **action** for the person doing it.

Beware Debates or Q&As
A reasonable presentation of plot points in an intelligent, balanced, logical manner is usually not how people talk. If your characters are engaged in the action of debating for personal reasons in that moment -- that's fine. But all too often, the writer is simply trying to feed us information by cutting it up and giving parts of it to different people. Don't do that.

Likewise, trying to get information out of someone can be a dazzling basis for a scene -- but don't just disguise an information-dump by interrupting it with leading questions. Make it an action, make it a scene.

Repetition Is (Usually) Death
Repeating an idea or saying the same thing in different words should almost always be cut. Except...

...sometimes people talk like that. It can reveal how they're thinking. If you have characters repeat themselves, do it because **they** need to repeat.

Also, there is a difference between repetition and escalation.

Someone saying the same thing over and over is dull, but putting new energy or meaning into an idea -- saying it with a new intensity or changing the form of it -- can work.

The key to escalation is often to make the rising intensity clear through changes in the phrasing or in the other character's responses.

Give Each Character a Voice

Character voice is more about attitude and style than anything else.

Are they crude, polite, mocking, gentle? Do they shape their sentences carefully, or ramble, or interrupt themselves? Do they ask a lot of questions? Do they generalize or philosophize? Are they blunt? indirect? Do they quote a lot, or analyze, or threaten?

Think about the world your character is from. Were they educated in some special field, or did they learn what they know on the streets? Which streets?

Every place, every job, every social group has its own vocabulary and way of speaking.

Jargon and slang can be useful. (Jargon is technical language in a type of work or activity, slang is casual language shared by a specific group.) Researching or making up jargon and slang can be fun. It creates a special world. But make sure it can be understood from the context, action and emotion.

Character voice is not an external layer you apply -- it comes from inside them, from who they are, how they feel and who they're talking to.

You speak differently to your boss than to your lover. You speak differently if you are trying to impress someone, or calm them down or stall them.

The voice, language, speaking style should come out of that relationship in that moment.

Word Order Is A Tool
What people start with or save for last tells you a lot about what they're thinking and feeling -- sometimes as much as the words themselves.

The audience grabs on to whatever comes first in a line -- but they get the biggest impact from how a line ends.

It's the opposite of what they teach you in school: in dialogue, you don't write a topic sentence that says everything, and then explain the details in the paragraph that follows. Hold the kick until the end.

Partly this is because dialogue is action, and once something has been put out there -- it requires a response.

Speeches, Monologues
A speech is a "little set piece". You're asking the audience (and the other people in the scene) to stop and listen -- so it really ought to be an event: a climax, a revelation, a turning point. You want a speech to be a little journey that the audience becomes aware of as it begins. Then you want to craft the rhythm and shape of the speech, in the style of the speaker to be a river, a wave, a rollercoaster ride -- with a distinctive, worthwhile, meaningful ending.

Listen
Listen to people talking. Explore, study, pay attention. Notice how your friends and family talk, people at your work or school or at the next table in a cafe.

Study The Dialogue In Movies And Shows You Love

Listen to it. Type it out. Get it away from the shots and the actors and just look at how it works, on the page.

Study Plays And Try Writing For Theater

It is an unbelievably good experience for anyone who wants to write any kind of scripts. Putting two people on a stage and building a scene just through their talk is the best dialogue writing class I know.

Watch some plays from different traditions, and maybe try to work with a theater group. It costs almost nothing to get some actors to workshop your play. Stage writing pushes you to see characters talking to each other as action.

Alternative Styles

I now want to briefly contradict everything I've been saying. There **are** other ways to approach dialogue.

What I'm describing in this chapter might be called "character-based" dialogue. It's the way most commercial stories are told in the current American/Hollywood system, and I think it's a useful skill to have.

But if you are drawn to a different style and it comes naturally to you -- it is worth exploring.

Many old movies and shows -- as well as anime, comic books and video games -- use more declarative dialogue, full of objective commentary and explanation. There are poetic styles of dialogue, or styles that follow the loose, sloppy real language of real people. And that can all work. There are different kinds of art.

If you have a voice, a style, that comes naturally and feels good: that's magic, take it seriously.

Sure, some people won't like it. But most art that matters, most influential or exciting art, has a distinctive voice. Many legendary screenwriters, from Paddy Chayevsky to Amy Sherman-Palladino, write every character talking pretty much in the same style...and it's great.

To me it seems worth gambling on your voice, if you feel it.

The main way you learn how dialogue works and get good at it is:

write a lot of dialogue

try it out on people

get people to read it out loud

and then do that again...and again

SUBTEXT

Subtext can scare new writers because it seems very technical, but it's really just the action behind the words.

Very often in life, people don't say what they mean. They want something, or think something, but they talk about it in an indirect way. That's subtext. It's the ideas or intent driving the lines and adjustments.

Subtext is not **your** secret meaning for the scene...it's **theirs:** what the character is privately thinking or feeling.

Actors love subtext because it gives them something to **do**, something to play when they're talking.

And audiences love it too -- they get engaged: playing the game, reading the people.

The trick to subtext is pretty simple: you need to know what the character is feeling, and what they are trying to accomplish.

Then look for ways to suggest it, express that -- without stating it directly.

The problem of subtext: how do you know that the audience will understand the unspoken?

Almost always we understand the subtext because the character's need, situation or opinion is shown to us in some earlier scene. For example, we have heard Jerry expound on his fear of people from the city -- so when Jerry's old school pal returns home for the holidays with his new fiancee from the city...even though Jerry is polite in conversation, we understand the anxiety behind his questions.

Or a character is having an affair, and their spouse comes home unexpectedly. The lover hides in the closet. From then on, the cheater's dialogue is heavy with subtext because they (and we) know the secret.

Subtext is not something mysterious or unknown: it's something we know, even though it is not said directly.

(I generally don't cite examples, because there are always too many possibilities and they stir up pointless debate, but: among the masterpieces of subtext-y dialogue, do check out *Butch Cassidy And The Sundance Kid* (1969), the first scene of *The Social Network* (2010), and the between-the-train-cars scene in *The Manchurian Candidate* (1962).)

EXPOSITION

There is no single, authorized definition of "exposition." This is mine:

exposition =
conveying information to the audience

Seen that way, a lot of writing for screens is exposition. It's not inherently bad. The audience **wants** information:

what's the plan?

what the problem?

who's that person?

what's in the box?

Exposition can be a **thrill** for the audience.

But so much of it is clumsy, confusing and undramatic. Often, it is forced inappropriately into dialogue:

```
"You remember when we were
kids, back in that terrible
neighborhood, and you wrote
that song?"
```

If these people grew up together, they **both know** the neighborhood was terrible. The only reason to say that is so the writer can tell the audience.

Many writers view exposition as homework or medicine that they just want to get out of the way. They dump a lot of information at once, often in its own scene where the story stops dead.

9 Ways To Make Exposition Better

Make It Dramatic Action

Exposition works when a character is trying to use it to get something or to make something happen. In life, people convey information in conversation all the time: they make reports, give orders, debate plans, explain situations to friends. They use information to distract, comfort, manipulate. They confess, gossip, brag. People use information as leverage in an argument and tell stories to back up their point.

Someone involved has to feel something about it. It ought to change something for them. Give someone a need to know.

Don't STOP For Exposition

Try not to build a scene in which the only thing happening is the exposition.

Find a situation where the exposition is either helping someone accomplish something or an obstacle to someone's action.

Or give people different intentions: one is trying to get something else done while the other wants to tell them something.

Or give your characters something else to do: people talk at work, while playing games, when they're under stress, when convincing, comforting or romancing each other, when they're brought together by a shared experience, activity or goal.

*(But don't just have them walk as they talk! A quick rant: "walk-and-talks" try to cover up exposition with Steadicam shots of characters walking while they talk. The theory being: let's give them something interesting to look at because talk is boring. These then devolved into just having the camera run in a circle around people while they're talking. Is it really a good idea to try to take the audience's attention **away** from what people are saying?*

How is that helping? Write a scene where the actors can play an interesting and dramatic moment in which the information matters! End of rant.)

Keep It Focused
Be clear on what you need to say. You have so little time and the ways you have to do it are so limited. Don't try to jam in too much at once.

Beware: Q & A's
The mere fact that one person is asking another for the information does not make it dramatic. Characters can certainly ask questions -- but it still has to be a scene. It must be something they need in the moment. Does something **change** because of this question-and-answer?

Beware: Cleaning Up
If you're thinking: *gee they might be confused about X...let write some lines to explain it.* See if, instead, you can go back and make the confusing thing not-confusing in the first place.

Beware: Recapping
Try to avoid having people tell each other something we already saw or that the listener already knows. There are times when recapping is a dramatic action, but be sure the character has a need to do so in that moment.

Find Other Ways
Think about ways to convey information that's not dialogue. Sure, they can be corny -- but they can also work:

> watching videos

> doing research in illustrated books or old newspapers

news reports

flashbacks

voice over

diaries

supernatural forces

Own it: "Explainer Scenes"

A lot of people in The Industry are terrified of scenes where someone simply tells us crucial information, but in fact these scenes can be satisfying and fun.

Among the great cinematic explainers:

ObiWan Kenobe (Alec Guiness) in *Star Wars: A New Hope*

Morpheus (Laurence Fishburne) in *The Matrix*

Harry Lime (Orson Welles) in *The Third Man*

Captain Koons (Christopher Walken) in *Pulp Fiction*

"X" (Donald Sutherland) in *JFK*

Louis (Danny Aiello) and Michael (Matt Craven) in *Jacob's Ladder*

Sheriff Bledsoe (Jeff Corey) in *Butch Cassidy & The Sundance Kid*

God in *It's A Wonderful Life*

Plus the narrator-heroes of *A Clockwork Orange, Mr Robot, Goodfellas, Fight Club, Annie Hall, Double Indemnity*...and almost every character in *Citizen Kane*.

Remember: the audience wants information, and "finding things out" is often a crucial goal of the characters.

Explainers can be a joy, a thrill.

Make It Interesting

make it poetic, emotional

give it the ol' razzle-dazzle -- make it a set-piece, a kick

make it a moment of larger insight, beyond the information

make it funny, or hard to get

give it to a character with a unique way of speaking, or someone unexpected or inappropriate

shape the scene, give it a punch line

break the exposition into pieces, so it's like putting together a puzzle or following a trail of breadcrumbs over several scenes

Homework: watch a movie you love and look for the exposition.

"ON THE NOSE" DIALOGUE

"On the nose" dialogue is:

characters saying exactly what they mean

dialogue that directly conveys information

Almost everybody tells you: don't do it. But these types of lines are not inherently bad.

The main gripe about on-the-nose: it can be boring, stating the obvious. But that's just bad dialogue. A character saying what they know, think or feel can be interesting, funny, unexpected or emotional.

A more legit problem: it makes the audience passive.

The audience wants to play -- interpreting, putting stuff together. On-the-nose dialogue should not simply spoonfeed the audience, but it can be a powerful way to give the audience those pieces they will put together for themselves.

Your on-the-nose line can also be a gift, a reward at the end of a dramatic process, a key that opens up the movie. Some of the best lines in cinema history -- the ones people quote, those zingers that perfectly phrase or summarize a moment or a story -- are on the nose:

> *Frankly my dear, I don't give a damn.*
>
> *Mrs Robinson, you're trying to seduce me.*
>
> *I see dead people.*
>
> *You don't understand. I coulda had class.*
> *I coulda been a contender. I coulda*
> *been somebody, instead of a bum, which is*
> *what I am, let's face it. It was you, Charley.*

These are some ways to make on-the-nose dialogue work:

Choose Your Nose

Don't do on-the-nose accidentally. Good on-the-nose means: you've made a choice, you know what's important at this moment and you're making it clear.

Not Too Much Nose

It's a powerful device: use it sparingly. Save it for when you really need it.

The bad version happens when you're on-the-nose about something that doesn't matter. Your on-the-nose line should be a gem, a revelation.

Make The Nose Dramatic

Not only does it have to matter to the audience, the person saying it has to have a strong feeling or reason to be plain, emotional, blunt.

The line should be an action, intended to provoke, confront, enlighten or steer someone.

Style Your Nose

An honest direct line can still have flair or style.

"Take apart" some movies and shows you admire: how much of what people say is on the nose? How do they make it work -- or not?

on-the-nose dialogue is a TOOL

know how it works --

when to use it and when not to

CAUSE AND EFFECT

Dramatic action makes something happen. That should have consequences. Ask yourself:

> what happens because of this action?
>
> what action made this event happen?
>
> do I have actions without a cause?

Ideally, the chain of cause-and-effect should be like a row of dominoes, a line one can follow with no gaps or cheating.

The task, then, is to prevent this from being predictable: to turn your line of dominos into a Rube Goldberg contraption (look it up) in which the logic of cause-and-effect is believable and yet the next event is in some way unexpected.

Assisting you in that task:

We Don't Have To Watch Every Step
Our attention can be directed elsewhere, so we return to the line only to discover something has happened (ideally with the chain-reaction visible in retrospect.)

Wait For It
Unlike an actual chain of dominos, an effect may be delayed. The line can be deliberately concealed for a while, by the characters or by the script's structure.

Uncertainty
It is rare that an action has only one possible effect. So a great deal of story tension comes from getting the audience to understand the possible effects, and to feel uncertainty as to which will happen.

People Are A Mess

Since many of your "moving parts" are people, not dominos, they can process events in unconventional ways and react unpredictably. They can be irrational, delusional or self destructive. Their actions spring from beliefs, feelings, patterns or personal qualities which, even if absolutely nuts, can be set up previous to their use.

The logic doesn't have to be anything we agree with -- but it does have to be meaningful to the character and consistent with what else we know about them.

ADJUSTMENTS

"Adjustment" is a method-acting term that's very useful for screenwriters. It refers to changes a character makes in their action during a scene.

Each character enters a scene with an intention -- a goal or objective, something they want -- and in the scene they do something to get it. But unless what they do works right away, they have to make a decision: what are they going to do, now that the first action didn't work?

Among the many possibilities:

> change the plan, take a new action
>
> double down
>
> choose a new goal
>
> try to correct or undo the first action

An example:

JOE
Betty, this company is
going to change the world.
Get in on the ground floor.

Joe asks Betty to invest in his new company. That's what he **wants** in the scene -- his objective: *get the money.* But!

BETTY
I'm sorry, Joe – I'm not
interested.

Betty rejects him, plainly and clearly. So Joe makes an **adjustment:**

>   JOE
>   You know, Betty, you
>   wouldn't even have any
>   money to invest if I hadn't
>   tipped you that WidgCo was
>   introducing Flex Widgets
>   five years ago.

He's still trying to do the same thing (get her to invest) but instead of hyping the company, he is now trying to make her feel obligated.

>   BETTY
>   I'm sorry, Joe - all our
>   money is tied up in Hugo's
>   stupid Alpaca farm.

Now Betty has made an adjustment: instead of just saying no, she's explaining why. So Joe makes a new adjustment: insteadof rethinking how to get his objective (get her to invest), he chooses a whole one -- now his goal is to make Betty feel bad, to soothe his own frustration or hurt:

>   JOE
>   You never liked me, did you?
>   You took advantage of my
>   connections but you don't
>   respect me. You're a leech
>   and you have bad taste in
>   shoes.

Even a scene without dialogue can have adjustments. For example, after Joe insults Betty, in desperation he goes to rob a bank:

```
INT. BANK - SOON AFTER
Joe enters, starting to pull a gun from his
coat pocket.

But he notices PROF. MAROON, who taught him
Ethics in college, waiting in line for a
teller.
Joe goes pale, puts the gun back in his
pocket and hurries out to the street.
```

Almost every good scene has an adjustment. Some can have a lot. There's no required number, but zero tends to make for boring scenes.

When characters make choices, they reveal their nature, thoughts and feelings right before your eyes -- which is what "makes a story happen."

The adjustment a character makes tells you about who they are and where they are in the story. In our scene with Joe and Betty we learned how easily he loses control, makes things personal, burns bridges.

Adjustments are where scenes get interesting.

Without them, scenes devolve down to stating information and then moving on to more information.

A simple tool, but they help you structure a scene and make the life in your script feel more complex and life-like.

Watch some scenes in something you like and look for the adjustments.

Become aware of the adjustments in your scenes -- build to them, make them clear, make them interesting, make them emotional.

SET PIECES

This is one of those important screenwriting terms that everyone throws around but no one actually explains.

I think this is a practical definition:

**a "set piece" is a scene or sequence
that offers a
NOTICEABLE,
HEIGHTENED
portion of
whatever the genre promises**

Set pieces are the scenes where the work does whatever-it is that made you want to see this type of story -- and they do it **very intensely.**

Set Pieces Deliver On The Hook Of The Project
In a horror movie -- it's the horror. In a thriller -- the suspense. In a musical...well, in a way set pieces in **anything** are like musical numbers: the moments when we lift off into the purest magic of this type of story.

It has nothing to do with budget or scale. "Who's On First" is two guys standing in front of a painted backdrop, but it's a major comedy set-piece. The opening scene of *The Social Network* is a dazzling set piece in which a couple sit at a table and talk for nine minutes.

You NEED Set Pieces
Set pieces are like stepping stones in a river. You can stand on them, and move from one to the next, and they'll get you across to where you're going.

Don't Go Too Long Without A Set Piece
There's no fixed number or timing but, as with stepping stones: don't make it too hard to get from one to the next.

A Set Piece Should Matter
Some people think a set piece should be "self-contained," implying that it's not related to the story or you could lift it out -- either of which would, I think, be bad.

It's a big intense sequence: it ought to **change** something, to be a turning point or important advance in the story. Even though it's unique and heightened, it still ought to be some form of dramatic action in the story.

I suspect what "self-contained" is trying to capture is:

A Set Piece Ought To Have A Beginning And An End
You should distinctly feel it starting and know when it's over.

A Set Piece Should Be NOTICEABLE
It should stand out, the audience should be aware they're in it.

What that is like depends on the genre and the type of scene -- but whatever it is: do it intensely. Make it original or unexpected or dazzling.

Set Pieces Should Be DIFFERENT From Each Other
Make sure you have a variety of them and each has a distinctive core or style. There should be a progress, a rhythm and a build, to your set pieces.

Figure out the magic of your type of story and make sure you're giving us intense, noticeable extravaganzas of that.

STAKES

When I started trying to define "stakes," I thought: *it's the urgency driving a character.*

It seems then: you should hype up the thing driving, pushing the character.

But that doesn't feel right. If you're increasing the power of something being done to the character, you're actually making the character **weaker.**

Focus on what the character is doing, the action they are taking.

What would make them take more action? If the thing they're trying to get becomes more important to them.

**stakes = how important
the "goal" or "thing they want"
is to a character**

When you want to raise the stakes, focus on how much, and exactly how, the goal is important to your character.

**make the thing they want
URGENT, CRUCIAL,
PERSONAL & EMOTIONAL
for your character**

If what-the-character-wants isn't really important to them, they are going to seem stupid to persist once the obstacles become substantial and intimidating.

(And your obstacles **should** be substantial and intimidating!)

When you get increasingly tough obstacles and a really urgent, emotional need to overcome them -- **that's** a story.

Some teachers advise thinking about the stakes as: *"What happens if they don't get it?"* -- but I feel stories are a bit less powerful when they're focused on trying to avoid something. Instead:

Tell Us WHY

Don't take what-they-want for granted -- even if it's money, power or sex. What does that **mean to them,** specifically, in their life and experience. Make us feel it in a unique, intense way.

We Can't Care About The Stakes If We Don't Know Them

Make sure the audience knows what the stakes are, and we need to know that pretty early in the story. Let us see what the characters care about at the start, so we can get involved. The "why" might come later, but:

> **let us know**
> **what to WANT &**
> **what to FEAR**
> **for your character**
> **early in the story**

Time Pressure

"I want to go to Italy one day," is less urgent than *"I want to go to Italy before this year is over."*

Not every story should have a literal ticking clock, but **do** give us a sense that this goal is important **now.**

Pile-On Plotting

It can be very tempting to raise the stakes by **adding** stuff: not only does the character have to stop a serial killer but also their lover is ill and they are trying to buy a sports bar.

That can be fine if all of those storylines affect each other, but having a character attend to two **unrelated** problems doesn't double the tension -- it divides it in half.

The main reason people come up with these pile-up plots is they're thinking in terms of what is **happening to** the central character, not what the character is **trying to do.**

to raise the stakes
ADD OBSTACLES,
not objectives

And emphasize cause-and-effect: *you need to solve problem B because it will get you closer to solving Problem A.*

Or *the solution of one problem, (or the attempt to solve it)* **causes** *a new and ideally worse problem.*

Intensify Your Obstacles
Make it hard for your character. If a spy has to save the world, but doing so barely ruffles their hair...the stakes aren't really that high.

Even if you're writing about an immortal invincible superhero, there has to be **something** that makes this particular set of events unexpectedly difficult for them.

Which brings up another **really important** aspect of stakes:

stakes are in the eye of the stake-holder

The stakes don't have to be life-or-death or saving-the world. In fact, big external stakes can lead you into lazy generic writing. What makes the stakes important is how the character feels about them. We can care a whole lot about who goes to the prom, or whether someone comes to terms with their difficult childhood.

Convey the character's need: why they feel it, how much they feel it. Make us understand and empathize, even if it's not our thing.

That's really the key:

make it personal
make it specific
make us care

...and the stakes will be high.

WITHHOLDING

One of the keys to telling a story is choosing what you don't tell the audience.

The audience looks for it. They want to **play.** They want to guess and dig, hope and fear for the characters, step into their shoes. Let them work on it, worry about it. Set them up to get the experience of discovery.

Bad storytelling tries to tell the audience everything. Good storytelling makes them ask: *what's going to happen?* **How** *is it going to happen?*

This requires writers to think about what exactly the audience should **not know** at any given time.

**choosing what to WITHHOLD
from the audience
is one of the most powerful tools in storytelling**

Because *"What's going to happen?"* does not mean: *"I have no idea what's going on!"*

It means, *"I want to see how the characters will act regarding the thing that just happened."*

Or more precisely: *"I have a set of things that I **want** to happen, but I **fear** these other things could happen."*

So think about what you want the audience to **want** to happen, and what you want them to **fear** will happen.

The More Specific You Are About Withholding, The Better

        I think there is a monster behind that door.

is better than

```
Monsters are scary.
```

and

```
I think the grotesque drooling reptilian
monster that I glimpsed outside a few minutes
ago is behind the door.
```

is even better.

If You Withhold TOO Much, The Audience Gets Bored Or Confused

If something arrives completely out of the blue, that creates a surprise but takes away the audience's ability to play.

the secret to withholding:
the audience needs to know (or suspect)
something is being withheld

To a certain extent, you want to make it evident that you are holding back. You want to **"clearly withhold"** specific information.

Think of a jigsaw puzzle: once you have put some of it together, you begin to hunt for the specific shape and color of the missing pieces.

Make sure they know enough about what-they-don't-know that they can actively engage in looking for it. The audience should be able to see the possible paths, and how they can go wrong.

The Power Of "How?"

Ideally, the audience is not sure the main character will get what they want. But often it's pretty clear they will. Especially in big commercial or genre stories, there really isn't any doubt the detective will solve the mystery or the rom-com couple will get together.

So often what the audience is **really** asking is:

> **"how will we get to the ending
> we know we're going to get?"**

That can be a great story. Make that **"how"** the fun, the game, the suspense. The path they're taking to that inevitable place can be where your story gets original or insightful.

Who Is Withholding?

An important decision you have to make when withholding:

> **is a CHARACTER keeping the secret
> or
> is the STORY ITSELF keeping something back?**

When you only show the villain's gloved hand putting poison in the coffee cup: you're telling the audience, *the storyteller or the story itself is withholding this information because we're playing a game.*

But if the character is withholding, they need to have a reason in the story. They have withhold because it helps them get what they want from the **other characters.**

And one last thought: the audience wants to play -- but they're counting on you to make the win **worth** something.

It can be small or quirky, but if you are withholding something: that thing is important. Make it emotional, an insight, a statement, a vision, a truth.

Make it matter.

THE INCITING INCIDENT

"Inciting incident" is a crappy name for a good thing.

a story is about someone trying to do something

the inciting incident is, simply, the reason

What makes your story begin? Why are the characters doing things **now**? Something must have happened.

It could be news, good or bad. It could be the result of something your main character has done, or some random event that has nothing to do with them. It could be long awaited or out of the blue.

Other than the fact that you probably need one, there really are **no rules** about inciting incidents. Especially not where it happens in your script. The idea that the inciting incident must happen on a particular page number is nonsense.

Most of the time, because it starts the story, the inciting incident likely to happen somewhere in the first part of a feature, or the first episode of a series.

Often it is after a few bits introducing us to the characters -- but sometimes the inciting incident is the very first scene.

Or it could have happened **before** Page 1. The main character doesn't know it yet, so we see them finding out. This can really hook us into the story, since we're with the character as they feel the impact of this event.

It's also possible to hold it off -- if there's enough interesting relevant stuff happening. In theory, you could follow unrelated storylines for half the story until then they come together and **that's** the inciting incident.

Starting From Normal?

Another incorrect "rule" is the theory that all drama begins with a stable situation which is then disturbed to start the plot. All stories then are about "trying to get back to normal."

Certainly, that is a story -- but **all** stories? No. Establishing normal is a perfectly fine structure, but it's not required.

The pre-story situation might in fact be discomfort or misery, and the story is about the struggle **not** to go back there. Or the events of the story change the characters in such a way that a whole new life begins for them at the end.

The problem with "establishing a stable normal" is that it can be dull -- when we should ideally be learning to love the main characters and invest in their desires or problems.

If you're going to start by establishing "normal," make the stable world precious, unique and interesting. Give us something specific to treasure when it is threatened or lost. Or play with the audience's awareness that "normal" is doomed; lay in, during the establishment of normal, disturbing elements or the seeds of the real story coming at us.

you almost always need an inciting incident

why is this story happening now?
something must have happened

what it is, when it happens, how it relates
....is up to you

FLASHBACKS

A surprising number of writers tell me they are afraid to use flashbacks, because their teachers insisted "flashbacks stop the forward motion of the story." And sure: a bad flashback will do that.

But flashbacks can be powerful storytelling tools. The key is to make them about dramatic action, instead of just information.

When you bring the past into the story it ought to be a revelation, a turning-point: everything that happens after it means something new because of what we now know.

It may reveal a character's motive, but the purpose of the flashback scene cannot be simply to inform. It should also be a part of present events: a discovery someone is making, an obstacle to the action, a tool someone is using.

**a good flashback
is an EVENT
in the PRESENT STORY**

Dramatically (and in life): the past is usually felt because something happens in the present to make us think about it, or because in the present moment, we need to use the past for some purpose.

In a good flashback you feel the past as present: it's happening in front of you, pulling you into the drama and character of both the past moment and its effect on the present story.

Within this essential use of the past, there are different types of flashback:

"Subjective" Or Character Flashbacks

A character is seeing or remembering or thinking about a past event. The memory happens **within** the story.

Make sure there's a reason -- a trigger, a problem, an event -- for that memory to come to them **at that moment.**

And it must have an effect on the person remembering:

give them useful information

push them to do something

serve as an obstacle to doing something

change something in the character or the story

"Objective" Or Audience Flashbacks

The movie itself is showing the past to us, the audience. The memory is not happening within the story, the characters are not remembering it.

Not every storytelling style allows for this. It tends to work best in a story with a bit of "narrative distance" -- if the story moves between storylines, or has some device like a narrator.

As a memory must matter to the characters, so this type of flashback has to make a difference to us in the audience. We now understand or know something which changes our thoughts or feelings about the story and the characters.

Fast Or Slow Flashbacks

"Fast" flashbacks are literally flashes -- very quick, often just images. They try to capture the experience of being in someone's mind when a memory hits. They often are subjective and happen within a scene.

"Slow" flashbacks leave the present to explore full scenes or sequences set in the past.

A Flashback Scene Is A SCENE

Make it **work** as a scene. Characters must be trying to do things. Actions must be taken, things should be revealed, changes should happen.

Often they are little stories in themselves: an incident with a beginning, middle and end.

A Flashback Is A Specific Moment.

If you're using a flashback to show a long history or general condition in the past, think about how to make that into moments. It can't be a summary. If you want to say *"The family was always happy until they had to move off the farm,"* it's got to be shown in a specific moment and type and action of happiness

Flashbacks Can Be Broken-up

The past events can be broken into segments and added to the story slowly, bit-by-bit. This is a great device to work in the past without stopping the story for too long. This kind of flashback even adds suspense to the present story.

The important thing to do with these is make clear that it's incomplete -- ending bits with a sense of uncertainty or hints of action still to come, possibly repeating sections when you come back to it, so the audience can pick it up and connect the dots.

Flashbacks Can Remind Us Of Events

Sometimes you flash back to events already seen in the story because the character is suddenly seeing that moment in a new way.

And sometimes you just do it to remind the character -- or the audience -- of some detail that's relevant to the present moment.

But! Flashbacks don't work for every story. Among the useful alternatives:

Characters Talking About The Past
A powerful, dramatic talk or monologue about the past can be a knockout moment.

A Mechanical Information Device
Internet searches, old film, video or audio recording, old photos or souvenirs, letters or diaries, looking up a news clipping or history book (often illustrated.)

Sure it's been done to death -- but used right it can be fun, refreshing or powerful.

"BACKSTORY"

"Backstory" is a screenwriting term for events that take place before the movie or show begins.

It may be motivating a character. It can define a character in the eyes of others in the story -- i.e. it's something someone (or everyone) knows about them, and affects how they are treated. Ideally, revealing it is a turning point.

But be careful: backstory can distance us from the urgency of the present.

If you're going to use backstory, make it part of the dramatic action between characters, now. The backstory dialogue or flashback should reveal the past because someone needs something, or is trying to do something, in the present. It should have an effect on the situation, the relationships, the action.

**the most important task
when working with backstory is:
making it a part of the story,
figuring out what what it is DOING
for the character**

PLOT TWISTS

What exactly is a plot twist?

If you are just talking about changes or surprising new information during a story -- every plot has a lot of "twists." A plot, basically, **is** "twists."

But it seems to me that when people talk about a "plot twist" now, they mean: **an event or revelation that makes you rethink your entire understanding of the story.**

This is not easy to pull off, and has a pretty high price in terms of sacrificing other values in your story. So the first question is: do you really need a plot twist?

Most great stories do not have them, in that sense.

Stories with plot twists are often shallow. Trying to jam in two entirely different ways of seeing the story means you only can give each a half-portion of storytelling time. This usually doesn't let you explore characters in depth.

Plot twist stories are especially vulnerable to spoilers and don't age well. If your work relies on the audience being dazzled by suddenly seeing the story in a whole new way -- what happens when they already know the secret?

In general: be wary of plot twists. A great one is great, but a mediocre plot twist story is a shallow, forgettable experience.

But if you're gonna do it -- do it right. Let's talk about how:

I think there are two different kinds of plot twist: The Shock or The Reveal

These are just **my names** for these ideas, and a reveal can be shocking or a shock can be revealing. Please don't get hung up on putting things in categories, that's not the point.

What I'm trying to get you to see: there is a difference between the story taking a whole new direction (which I'm calling a "shock") and seeing the story in a new way (which I'm calling a "reveal.")

The Shock Twist

A new, unexpected event takes the story in a radically new direction. It substantially changes the goals, tone or subject of the story.

(Examples include *Sinners, From Dusk Til Dawn, The Crying Game* and *Psycho.*)

Shocking story-changes-in-the-middle twists are rare, because they are a risk. If the audience really likes one half, and the other half is radically different, they can easily end up feeling bored, cheated or pissed-off.

The Reveal Twist

New information makes you re-think elements of the story that you believed you understood.

Like: *"oh my God -- her side of the story is in a different time than his!"* or: *"oh wow, that character only existed in the other character's mind!"*

This type of twist has a famous sub-genre: The Twist Ending, in which the very last thing that happens makes you look back on the whole story in a new way. When these work, they're great. *The Prestige, The Planet Of The Apes, The Sixth Sense* and *The Usual Suspects* do it well.

But in general, twist endings are hard to pull off. You have no room to work after, so it it's often unsatisfying.

Also, the audience can't feel retroactively. A cool twist won't help if we have spent much of a story bored, frustrated or indifferent. We have to be truly engaged in the "wrong" story (see below.)

A Twist Needs To Feel "Unexpected And Yet Inevitable"

Which means, in mechanical terms: it has to "pay off" elements that were set up, but in a way we don't see coming.

The set-up should register with the audience when it happens, but be understood as something other than a set up. This is mostly accomplished through the essential magician's trick: **misdirection.**

> make the set-up seem unimportant or even ridiculous

> other things should be busier, more colorful, more hyped

> have the set-up be something taken-for-granted by the characters

> affiliate it with a character who is not taken seriously

> "bury" it in a list or group

> make it seem like it is over: been completed, or failed

> have it serve two purposes (give it different use or meaning to different characters)

A Plot Twist Requires A "Convincing Wrong Version"

The audience has to believe that the wrong version **is** the story. You want them to invest in and care about it.

Rushing through it or making it too simple means your audience will tune out before the twist.

Making the false story real and misdirection also help with a serious danger of plot twists:

You Don't Want Your Main Character To Be Dumb

Your main characters will not see the twist coming. Work to make the audience feel the characters are making an honest mistake for an understandable reason.

Let The Characters (And Audience) React To The Twist

Give them some time to feel it, to process it. If possible, let them acknowledge within the story that what's happening is shocking, unsettling, maybe even unfair.

Break Your Plot Into Small Steps

Twists get more convincing when they are not just the content of a single scene. There is something about laying events out in steps, over time, that helps draw the audience in. By building the twist in several scenes, you repeat crucial information and help the audience grasp and enjoy the "game."

The Signal/Trigger/Reveal Should Be Clear and simple

It may refer to a complicated set of acts or meanings, but the way we learn about it should be a simple sentence or a clear visual clue.

You can't EXPLAIN a plot twist -- it has to HAPPEN

Often a plot twist is someone telling someone something -- but that doesn't mean you're explaining the twist. The telling itself should be a dramatic action, a story event with an effect on a character.

And finally:

A Plot Twist Ought To Say Something

Make it worth the disorienting experience by having it play out, embody, or confront characters with a revelation, an insight into the people or themes.

You still have to do everything a good story does, within the limits of the twist and even if the twist doesn't work.

Create characters, events, themes and feelings that people will care about even if the twist has been spoiled or watching it a second time.

make it matter to the characters
make it real
make it a story we care about even without the twist

STORY VS PLOT

I find it useful to define "story" as **what happens** and "plot" as the **form in which the story is told.**

Story is the experience of the characters: what happens to them and how they experience it. Like their lives, it is chronological.

Plot is how you tell us that story: the choice of what you show the audience, and when. Do you switch from one person's experience to another or stay with one? Do you tell it in the order it happened? Is there a narrator?

The same story can be told via different plots, and there can be many stories running within a plot.

In the plot you decide what is important, whose story or point-of-view are you following in each scene, the order in which you reveal key information.

Writing the story and the plot are two separate tasks. In theory: story comes first since you can't figure out the plot until you know the story -- but really you often go back and forth.

Story and plot are both essential. Neither can really exist without the other. They are a balance of content and form.

The key practical use of this idea is: **when you have a problem or a decision to make know which you're trying to solve.** Is it in the story, or the plot?

It's a simple idea but I think you'll be surprised how useful it is when you get all tangled up trying to figure out your script.

**story is what happens
plot is how you tell it**

STORY PHYSICS

This is not real physics, but it's inspired by Sir Isaac Newton's Laws Of Motion, which he supposedly figured out watching balls on a billiard table:

A ball is not going anywhere unless something knocks into it. Once it gets knocked into, it rolls in a certain direction and keeps going that way until it gets where it's headed or it knocks into something else.

This is like a character in a story:

> a character will not go into motion unless they are acted upon by a force (which can be internal -- a desire or feeling -- or external -- an event or other character.)

> once a character is in motion, they will keep going in that direction unless struck by another character or force.

> (Actually, inertia will also slow it to a stop -- so don't let that happen: make it move with enough energy.)

This is a simple idea, but useful. Ask:

> what made them start moving?

> what direction are they going in?

> what gets in their way or knocks them off course?

SET UP AND PAYOF

A huge amount of screen storytelling is setup-and-payoff.

It's a simple principle: we expect that if something is in a story, it has a purpose, it will be used, it will have meaning.

(Chekhov used his famous gun to illustrate the idea.)

Writers can take advantage of this: when you put something in your story -- you create an expectation, a tension, a puzzle, a curiosity.

This is especially enjoyable when you introduce something -- a character, object, ability, idea or location -- with one apparent purpose or meaning, and then later use it to accomplish or resolve something that was not the original or obvious use.

But even when you're not creating a twist or surprise, the basic principle is important: the audience can't enjoy the use of something when they are just learning of its existence. If you want them to feel a dramatic satisfaction or kick, you need to establish the thing that will be used, earlier.

Therefore, you often want the audience to recognize the set-up. Sometimes it is mentioned or seen repeatedly. This creates a fun form of tension: *I know this will be used -- but when, how?*

But in other circumstances, you may want to "bury" the set up: get it in, but disguise it or distract from it.

The **way** you set things up will depend on the style and story of each script. But whether it's hidden or obvious -- "setup and payoff" is central to storytelling.

(In a sense, the basic question of a story (*what does the main character want? will they get it?*) is the setup. The ending is the payoff.)

Look at anything you've got in a story. Think about how it is set up, how it pays off.

PATCHING

"Patching" is my name for adding an element to a script to cover a hole or solve a problem.

It's usually not a great idea.

Sometimes it's just a bit of dialogue, which can be fine:

```
              RUFUS
     Why don't we just take
     the elevator instead of
     climbing up the side of the
     building?


              GRUMPY
     Because the elevator
     has unbeatable security
     cameras.
```

But writers are often asked to "add a scene" to answer a question that someone **fears** an audience may ask -- so the story just stops dead while we justify, rationalize or explain.

The longer or more elaborate the patch, the more likely this becomes. The patch can even call attention to something that would otherwise have passed unnoticed.

People in The Industry tend to forget this: they think their response is the same as an audience's -- but in fact they are scared the script will fail, and therefore hyper-alert to obscure rules and formulae. Also (even though it contradicts their fear of the analytical audience) they are constantly worried that the audience is dumb, so they want everything explained.

Warning signs that you are patching: introducing a problem and solving it in the same scene, or having a scene or bit of dialogue which has no consequences.

A good way to check if the problem you want to patch is really worth it: *is this a concern* **for a character?**

If it **is** a concern of a character, and it's important -- if you **must** patch:

Make The Patch A Dramatic Incident
Make it something the characters have to figure out or accomplish or overcome. Have it reveal or develop a character. Something should change when it happens.

Try Not To Add Characters Or Scenes For A Patch
Use what you have. What characters or locations or elements already in the story can you use to solve this problem?

Try To Give It Some Flavor Or Style
Make it funny or offbeat or clever.

And most important:

Keep Patches Small
Ideally, at worst it will feel like driving over ice: the wheels may spin uselessly or slide sideways for a beat -- but then they get their traction back and we're on our way.

GENRE

A genre is simply a category. It's a way to sort artworks by style or subject matter. Literary critics use the concept to study common themes or stylistic elements, variations and meaning in different periods, etc.

Distributors and marketing departments use genre categories to help customers find what they want -- so for them: genre is the shelf, the page, the menu that the product is on.

But literary theory and marketing are looking at work that already exists. Writers are creating something that **doesn't exist yet.**

And so for writers:

genre is a set of EXPECTATIONS

For example, in the detective genre, the story almost always begins with someone bringing the detective a new case. Westerns often end with a showdown between two characters in an empty street. In a boxing movie, there are usually gamblers or criminals who want to fix the fight.

A genre is a bountiful warehouse of story events, plot twists, character types, settings, attitudes, themes and emotions.

The audience goes in knowing them -- and wanting to see what you're going to do with them.

You can **use** those expectations, fulfilling them or pushing them to new heights -- or you can undermine and question them, to startle and challenge the audience.

Looking at genre this way is an amazingly useful tool.

Know Your Genre

Every genre has its own eras, sub-genres, classics and masters. It gives you characters, themes and plot elements to use or twist or reinvent, a set of ideas and feelings to explore.

Get to know that stuff -- not just the hits but the history, the obscure variations. Look into books, podcasts, articles and essays about your genre.

Watch as much of it as you can. Then: break down some examples you really love, make outlines, puzzle out the mechanics and style and vision.

Satisfy The Genre

Be sure your script is providing at least **some** of the expected elements.

Remember that "genre" exists partly because human beings have a serious hunger for the familiar: children love to hear stories over and over. We crave the ritual of having the same elements played out in different disguises.

Ignore that at your peril -- but also:

Rethink The Genre YOUR Way

We also crave novelty -- something unexpected, even shocking. So while you need to respect and satisfy the genre, you also need to bring something new.

What's **your** take on this genre? What are you bringing to it?

be ORIGINAL within the FORM
CREATIVE within the RITUAL

Genre Blending And Genre Bending

"Genre Blending" is mixing two genres -- like a romantic comedy western.

"Genre Bending" is working within a genre but doing things that defy its conventions.

Generally, The Industry resists bending or blending genres: you piss off the purists and can confuse the audience. However, when it works, bending or blending can make legendary hits that change the genre forever.

(Sometimes, the bending and blending are successful enough to create a new subgenre, like "horror comedy.")

Genre-bending or genre-blending are great ways to make your work powerful and alive, but they can be harder to sell. Go in with your eyes open.

There Is No Official List Of Genres

"Independent film" was just a method of financing and distribution, but now it's a genre. Is "action" a genre? What would define "action movie": the type or style of action, the amount of action? A war movie or a crime movie likely has action -- but war movies and crime movies are also genres themselves.

Plus: some people call things genres -- like "coming of age" or "fish out of water" -- that I think are just types of stories. They could play out in different genres.

Some movie stars or directors might be thought of as genres: "a John Wayne movie" or "a John Waters movie."

Don't get too hung up on any of this.

Just get deep into the genre you want to work in and you'll figure out what you need to know.

My main message on genre: you're not a professor or a store. You're a writer, creating something new -- and genre gives you a set of tools, a landscape to play in.

All you have to add is the magic ingredient: you.

KNOW Your Genre
SATISFY Your Genre
RETHINK Your Genre YOUR way

THEME

Sooner or later, every writer will face a terrible question about each project:

What is this ABOUT?

Not just: what happens -- but what do those events **mean**? What ideas and emotions does this story explore?

In English class, they called this the theme. You could also call it the "vision" or "message."

The most important thing you need to know about theme is:

your theme is not a topic
it is a statement ABOUT a topic

You can't just write about "love." That's too big, too general. You can only write about love by having a "take" on it, a point of view:

"*love stinks*"

"*even unrequited love is good*"

"*love requires sacrifice*"

"*love keeps us young (or helps us grow up)*"

It can also be in the form of a question:

"*can you be in love with more than one person?*"

"*does love last?*"

But since your ending is usually going to involve a choice being made or an act having a consequence...you do imply an answer.

Does Your Story HAVE To Mean Something? Can't It Just Be Entertainment?

No. Because "meaning" and "entertainment" are not in conflict, they don't rule each other out.

The "just entertainment" theory is mostly put forth by people who don't want to be held responsible for what they do *("sure we killed all those characters who are in one specific demographic group...but it's just entertainment,")* or creators and consumers who got bored out of their minds in school being told "art" has to be analyzed -- so anything fun must not be art.

But if the 20th Century taught us anything, it's that the difference between "high art" and "low culture" is a class thing, not an art thing.

"Just entertainment" does not exist, because:

**the audience is going to
find meanings in your work,
whether you want them to or not**

Human beings **interpret**. We figure out the world, it's how we survive.

Furthermore, you are putting in meaning whether you know it or not.

**every story makes a statement
when someone takes an action
that has consequences**

So we learn: in the world of this work, **this** type of behavior will solve problems, but **that** type of plan will fail. *Crime does not pay* or *being true to yourself is how you succeed.*

These "statements" are often unintentional or cultural assumptions the creators carry without being aware of it. And yet: there they are, in the work.

Why Bother?

If the audience will interpret your work no matter what: why not just let them, and create without giving any thought to what you're saying?

Two reasons:

**if you don't think about
what you're saying,
you might be saying something awful**

and

**if you know what you're saying,
you can say it better**

So: how, exactly, do we find and work with a theme?

Name Your Theme

Write it out, as a simple statement. This is just for yourself. Maybe you'll tell people down the line, maybe you won't.

What If You Don't KNOW What Your Theme Is?

The theme is already in your story. A theme is not a separate thing you drop on top of a story so people can point to it and pass a test. Your theme is built into this feeling-and-idea-machine you're inventing.

Think about your story. Is it about love, war, science, jealousy, cooking?

Then ask:

what am I **saying** about that?

what do I **want** to say?

what is **something** I think is true about this stuff?

These are big questions. Look at what happens in your story. What does that mean to you? Think about what you think. Listen to what you feel, your honest instincts. This takes practice.

It doesn't have to be the final answer for the world. It doesn't have to be important or solve everything. It just has to be something you think is true.

Brainstorm. Try versions. Take your time, and then try again.

There are no rules for a theme. There is no right or wrong. And it's personal: different people will find different meanings in the same story.

Look at your unfinished work. Let it show you what it is.

Choose One Central Theme
If it's good, your script will be "about" **many** things.

Choose **one** to make central, most important.

You will have so many questions as you write. This choice becomes the core answer which organizes all the other choices.

Being able to say "this is what it's about" -- to articulate the core of the story -- is a useful skill, especially in a complicated, collaborative art like screenwriting. You will be working with people who have different concerns, who want to push the script to be about different things -- and at any given time, for all sorts of reasons, something may have to be cut or changed.

At those moments, you need to know what matters most.

Does A Theme Need To Be Original Or New?

Nope. If you have something new to say, or something that is rarely said -- absolutely, say it.

But a new story that illuminates an old truth can be a wonderful thing. Some people would argue truths are inherently **not** new, that truth is timeless wisdom.

Does A Theme Need To Be "Universal"?

When people in The Industry talk about "universal themes," they really just mean getting a large share of the market. Human beings share many emotions and experiences, but every place and time, every culture and group (and person!) has a different way of understanding them.

Art is always specific. You can only create a **particular** scene or character or story. We capture and communicate what is shared by creating something distinct and individual.

Do You Have To State The Theme In The Script?

Think of your script as an upside-down pyramid: the "point" at the bottom is supporting that big flat surface on top, all those words on all those pages.

You don't want the "point" all over the surface, but to be under everything -- maybe stated only once, or maybe not at all.

If you decide to put it in the dialogue: a lot of making dramatic writing smart and meaningful is about figuring out whose mouth to put an idea in, and when.

What character can see that truth? Why? What happens to allow that? If it is not the central character -- who are they hearing it from? What does it do to them to hear it? Sometimes the person saying it doesn't understand how valuable the words are. Also good: having wisdom come from an unexpected person.

But there is also real power in **not** just handing it to the audience. They get an extra magic when they see your theme **play out** in the story for themselves without being told.

The unspoken can be, admittedly, a tough sell. Putting your theme in the dialogue -- if it's done well -- probably does help you in The Industry.

It's a choice. Do what you do best, write what you want to see.

If you **do** put your theme into the dialogue: find an emotional, catchy or poetic way to say it. Maybe make it an impassioned speech or a powerful moment.

Where In The Story Does It Go?
If you put it in early, we can think about it as the story unfolds. But then have it come up as a question or have it be put to a test by events, leave a bit of uncertainty -- otherwise the story's kind of over.

If you want it near the end: watch out for turning it into a "moral of the story" after the action is settled. The audience likes a good quotable line, but they hate being spoon-fed a lecture on something they already felt.

The main thing: make any statement of the theme a dramatic action. Have a character **need** to say it to someone who has an emotional plot-related **need** to hear it at that moment, or let the characters **discover** it in a way that matters to them.

If It's Not In Dialogue, How Is The Theme Seen?
Meaning comes from seeing an idea unfold, enacted

dramatically through the arc of a character, a crucial image, or a climactic action.

Make it into a problem for the characters. Play it out in the actions they take. Make it **happen**-- make us **feel** it.

Even when it is enacted in a dramatic moment, theme is a feeling or idea carried by the whole work. It's alive in the characters, the dialogue, the plot, the world.

Your Script Should EXPLORE A Theme, Not Just Say It Once
While your script may make a statement, that does not mean it should be easy or reductive.

Your story and characters should question it, offer alternatives, play out variations. Give different characters real voices on all sides of your idea, so the audience has to think about it and make choices.

Every story has a theme: the lowest comedy, the sappiest romance, the most escapist fantasy. Taking that seriously heightens the story's power -- and gives everyone a reason to show up for work.

You're putting something into the big pile of stuff in the world, asking someone to read it, watch it, take it into their mind and their life.

So say something you've really thought about and honestly feel or believe. Raise a challenging question. Talk about something that **matters to you.**

REVELATION

One way to understand the job of storytelling: arranging events to create a place for revelation.

I don't mean a bit of news or a plot turn -- I am talking about a moment of insight and emotional power.

**a revelation is a moment of of INSIGHT -
a statement or vision -
regarding an essential or powerful
feeling or idea in the story**

Revelation is one of the main reasons we have narrative art. It's not easy in our lives to break through the everyday and let ourselves really **see** and **feel**. Stories can bring us to those moments.

But that kind of experience doesn't "just happen." That's the tricky thing about making art: you have to use form and technique to be spiritual and emotional.

**a revelation is NOT just a
slogan, explanation or lesson**

It **may be** something you can pull out and quote -- but it can't just be dropped into the story, disconnected and stand alone. Even if the revelation is something as simple as: "people need a little entertainment" (as in *Sullivan's Travels*) -- it should be an emotional, meaningful moment (as in *Sullivan's Travels*).

**there may be several revelations in a story
but usually one is most important
it usually comes toward the end**

It is possible to start with the revelation and then explore the impact, details and complexities for the rest of the story. But it's hard to keep that structure from feeling like it's winding-down as it goes on.

**a story is not just
UNFOLDING FROM something
it's BUILDING TO something**

Thinking in terms of revelation helps you prioritize everything in the script, as you organize your story around getting to that intensity.

**revelations should be set up, prepared-for,
built into the structure**

How Does The Audience GET This Revelation?

How does this vision, this idea come into the story in an action or a scene?

If it's spoken: who says it, why, how? If it's visual: what image or act embodies and expresses it?

Is this a revelation for a character, or just for the audience? Either can work. Some very powerful stories give us an insight that the characters are not able to see themselves.

If a character is going to have this revelation, you need to construct their story to give them the need and the ability to convincingly see it or say it. Perhaps make it a driving question or goal for them, set up a problem that will be solved by the revelation, or put the revelation at the heart of a conflict between characters with opposing visions.

If the character is **not** getting the revelation, how does the audience get it? What is the moment, the action?

Usually A Revelation Is Best When It Is Simple

When you put all this work into building to a revelation, it's tempting to slow that moment down, explore the idea in detail, really talk it out -- but it's usually best to be very simple.

It often needs to be only a single sentence, an image, a gesture.

The challenge is making that small event powerful, clear, somewhat unexpected and graceful.

You spend time and effort building up to it so you can keep it simple and the audience is ready to take it in.

Poetry And Magic

I personally think it's okay to make the revelation a bit unbelievable. Maybe the moment is a little too lucky, or the person saying it is a bit too poetic, or it refers to something legendary, mythic or spiritual.

I think even in the most realistic stories, we don't mind a bit of magic.

Revelations Of A Place, Time Or Idea

Sometimes the revelation isn't in a scene or a statement at all -- it's the story itself, exploring a time or place, a culture or group or type of work. Even if these works have a traditional plot or specific moments of insight, the driving purpose of their stories is an effort to capture (reveal) the truth or reality of a community, a time or place, a way of living.

For example: *Nashville, Treme, Day For Night, Nomadland, Witness, A Chorus Line, Euphoria, The Sopranos, Do The Right Thing* or *Atlanta*.

The Content Of Revelations

I believe if your revelation is just what you think will sell, or a cliche formula, it's going to feel hollow and be quickly forgotten.

ideally, a revelation will tell us
something we never knew

or

describe something we have felt or thought
but never really stopped to honor or understand

or

remind us of some truth that has become
worn, commonplace, forgotten...
and give it renewed power

The most important thing about a revelation is you feel like it's a truth.

It doesn't have to be the one-and-only-truth, it doesn't have to solve everything.

It can be a small truth, a common everyday truth, even a private truth.

Just make it something you believe in. Keep it real.

DRAMA vs NARRATIVE

At the dawn of time, "storytelling" was just that: around a fire or in a ritual space, a storyteller told the audience about the people in the story, what they felt and what they did. And it was good.

But then at some point, someone (reportedly Aeschylus, but who really knows) said: "What if we have different people acting and speaking as the people in the story? What if they play it out, right in front of us?"

Which was also good. Just in a different way.

It's easy to take this for granted, but now storytelling has two modes, two forms:

narrative = a narrator TELLS YOU the story

drama = performers ACT OUT the story

They're both marvelous but each has unique problems.

The Main Problem For Narrative: How To Keep It From Getting Boring
All you've got is your voice, so if you're not careful, it turns into: *this happened, then this happened, then this happened.*

But the trade-off is you can **do anything**. You are not restricted to the limits of time, space, actors, budget...even physical reality.

Meanwhile drama has two central problems:

Problem #1 For Drama: Production And Performance
You have limited time and limits (physical and financial) on

what you can make happen in front of people's eyes.

Problem # 2 For Drama: How To Make It Believable

Since all you've got to work with is the dialogue in the moment of the scene, it can be hard to make it convincing that these people are saying all the stuff you need them to say.

But the trade-off for that is seeing it happen. We're not just being told about it. This has astonishing power.

screen stories are BOTH NARRATIVE & DRAMA

They narrate: the camera, production design, editing and sound steer what you see and who you follow. But they also play out stories in scenes between actors, often talking.

So screenwriting requires writers to solve the problems of both

Ways To Keep Narrative From Being Boring

Make It News

Scenes should be about something important, something we don't know, something that changes the situation for the characters.

Don't show every step of a journey or process. Get to the new thing.

Vary The Method

Change up how you tell the story, scene to scene. Tell it close, tell it far. Have someone tell it. Have us see it without words. Put the news at the end of a scene, build to it. Start a scene with the news and show the effect it has.

Provide An Insight

Make the moment meaningful. Make it true. Make an argument. Make it about more than just the story -- make it about our world, our lives. Give it a feeling.

Ways To Make Drama Convincing

Give Each Person In The Scene A Dramatic Action

Give each character something they want and make scenes play out between two or more people.

Give It Urgency

Make the thing they want important to them, and the obstacle significant.

Give Each Person A Distinctive Voice

Give everyone their own language and verbal style -- not just a way of talking, a way of **thinking**: an opinion, an agenda, a manner.

Make It Move

Don't just let people debate or explain -- keep it moving, make things happen.

WORLD BUILDING

"World Building" is a catch-phrase associated with sci-fi and fantasy, but everything you write takes place...in a place.

when you tell a story, you are building a world

We don't often think about this because we assume a lot of worlds -- especially the ones we live in, or have seen in movies or shows -- don't need "building."

But look at some "known worlds": the police, the American high school, the military, office work. Think about how many different physical, emotional, social and intellectual versions you've seen.

The way we present the characters' world colors the audience's experience. If you just assume it's "known," you're giving up an important part of your creative tool box, and likely relying on cliches.

Before we go any further, though -- if you write because you love world-building, you should know:

Screenplays Are The WORST Possible Medium For World Building

Screen stories lure us with dense visual and aural experience. They feel like life, full of information.

But all those detailed ships, goblets and maps in your favorite movies and shows: the screenwriter didn't design those. It's not your job. The production designer and director and all of the amazing departments do that. And **none** of them said: "oh great, the writer did our job for us -- let's just forget about being artists and experts and do what they say!"

When you detour into the history or texture of people or places in a script, you're derailing the story. A narrative screenplay is remarkably spare and restrictive. You just don't have space in a script to really build a world.

If you truly want to build a world in detail: consider another art form. Write a book, make a graphic-novel zine, design an indie videogame Larp or create some new recombinant form that you invent.

That said, let's get into what you actually can do to build a world in a script:

Should You Build the World First?
I'd say no. Build it over time while you work out your story, characters and ideas.

Forget Originality
There is no such thing as an "original world." Even the most ground-breaking imaginative worlds come from a reworking and combination of material from other sources.

I think this quote from Jim Jarmusch says it better than I ever can:

> *"Select only things to steal from that speak directly to your soul. If you do this, your work (and theft) will be authentic. Authenticity is invaluable; originality is non-existent. And don't bother concealing your thievery -- celebrate it if you feel like it. In any case, always remember what Jean-Luc Godard said: "It's not where you take things from -- it's where you take them to."*

Instead, focus on:

Vision

The unique coherent meaning and emotion of your world. What does this world **tell** us? What **feelings** and **thoughts** does it provoke?

Those are the screenwriter's job -- what you bring that everyone else, doing all those other jobs, rely on:

> **the VISION of your world-building**
> **creates, steers & inspires**
> **the filmmaking work**
> **you can't do in the script**

Style

Your particular taste, your influences and choices.

Be creative and adventurous in your world-scavenging! Take from history, science, philosophy, biographies, journalism and other art forms like painting, photography, music.

And especially from your experiences, interests, observations and feelings.

Craft

The ways you use the mechanics of the art form to make your choices powerful, coherent and meaningful. Gathering cool stuff is not, unfortunately, the whole job. You need to do something with it:

Modify

Mess with what you take from the world, change it. Take things apart and give the pieces a twist. Make them fit your ideas and style.

210

Blend

Mixing stuff up is an art: juxtaposing, echoing, matching, contrasting, blending and layering the stuff you add to your world. Get comfortable playing with selections and proportions.

Create Texture

When people talk about "texture" in a screen story they usually mean visual style and production design -- but the unique and important "world texture" in a script includes:

group and personal relationships
political and social organization
beliefs / ideas / philosophy
atmosphere and feeling
physical elements / limits / realities
behavior / customs / rules / manners

The script itself also has a "texture": your writing style, attitudes and values -- the ways your characters talk, how you describe the places, people and actions.

Imagine Living In Your Invented World

I hesitate to offer this tip because it can become a rabbit hole you never want to leave...but: spend some time imagining the everyday experience of living in this world.

Think about the things your characters do in the story: imagine the physical reality and the emotional experience. Write down what you see and hear and feel.

The lifesaving trick to balance diving-in-deep like that is:

Prioritize Your World Building Around Your Story

A classic image of The Industry we write scripts for is the "backlot street": a detailed realistic row of building fronts that have no buildings behind them.

You may imagine the world behind that false front -- but if your story and characters don't go in there, how can we know about it?

In our real lives, we unconsciously select what we see and hear. Look around you right now, at something specific: a coffee cup, a chair, a part of the floor. Notice how your eyes "tune out" what's around it. You can't focus on everything. At any given moment some things are more important, and our brains automatically put them into proportion to our interests and feelings.

The story is how we will experience your imaginary world.

Details only exist when they're relevant to the story, a part of your character's lives in the relatively few scenes we get to see. Think about **why** you're working out exactly how the transit system works. If we never see anyone use it in your script, make sure you're not neglecting the stuff we actually need to know.

when you are world-building in a script, ask two questions:

what is the USE of this item in the story?

what is the MEANING of this item in the story?

WRITING STYLE

There is a standard, correct screenwriting format. Screenwriting **style**, however? Dealer's choice, anything goes.

What do I even mean by "style"? My definition:

screenwriting style =
your STORYTELLING VOICE

(how you use the words on a page
to steer & engage the reader's mind)

No one is going to buy a script for the writing style. I think of it like vehicle engineering: sometimes you want it to be snazzy, but mostly it should be effective yet invisible.

It's useful to start by recognizing that a screen script is a unique art form.

a script is
a set of instructions
and
a description of an imagined movie
and
a sales document
and
a narrative reading experience
ALL AT ONCE

Being able to balance all of those things is what makes a good script.

There is no rule for what proportions of those elements you should use, but there is one principle I believe is most important:

the unique, crucial job of a script:

**create the CHARACTERS
and tell their STORY**

**use your style to make the reader feel
like they're reading about
stuff happening to real people
as they read it**

I believe the main task of style in a script is to "make it happen" for the reader.

In practical terms: how do we **do** that?

Care About Words On A Page
You are trying to convey people, places, events, ideas and feelings only using words. Words are your palette of colors, your scale of notes.

So the choice of words and the order you put them in, how you break them into sentences and paragraphs is **really important**. Start to care about that.

This does not mean using proper or formal language. You get no points in screenwriting for sounding like you're in school. This is about emotions, ideas, flow, impact.

Guide the mind with your words.

Sentence Structure
Sentence structure and paragraph breaks organize thoughts -- gives them priority and reveals them in time.

Think about the rhythm, change it up. Shape your sentences to steer the mind and tell us what to focus on:

```
John is holding the gun.  He leans against
the door frame, breathing heavily.

John leans against the door frame, breathing
heavily, holding the gun.
```

Neither is right or wrong. They simply present a different feeling, a different moment.

Use As Few Words As You Can

In general use the fewest, most active, most emotional words.

Extra words get between the reader and the reality of the events unrolling sentence to sentence.

Short, simple sentences. You can even use sentence fragments (as I just did at the start of this paragraph!)

Don't waste words on the obvious:

```
Fred walks over to the gang members. He stops
when he reaches them, and begins to taunt
them.

Fred walks over to the gang members, and
begins to taunt them.
```

Use Active Verbs
Avoid "is" and "was." Describe actions more than states of being.

Instead of "Rose is standing in the corner":

```
Rose lurks in the corner
Rose hangs back in the corner
```

```
Rose waits in the corner
```

Take advantage of the fact that scripts are are written in the present tense. Make things **happen:**

```
He walks into the cabin.
She shows her cards to the other players.
```

How Much Detail?
Less is more. Sometimes you do "paint with words" to inspire a vision in your collaborators -- but it is rare for anyone to want a long, detailed description of anything in a script.

Scripts are like trying to convey the experience of riding a raft down a river: too little detail -- nobody knows what's going on. Too much detail -- it doesn't move, you lose the flow and the pace.

Tell The Story
Describe things that help us care about the people and what they're doing.

Try not to step out of the moment. Talking about what the camera is doing interrupts the magic spell of being with these people in their world.

Use Your Writing Style To SUGGEST Cinematic Effects
Your language can "steer" the reader to imagine the screen effects you really should try not to describe.

For example, when you write:

```
The watch on his wrist ticks past midnight.
```

We "see" that as a close up. Or:

```
The wagon train crosses the plains under the
cloudless sky.
```

-- will likely make us "see" a wide shot.

A paragraph break is like a mental "cut":

```
Bill picks up the folder and Susan sighs,
shakes her head.
```

-- feels different from:

```
Bill picks up the folder.

Susan sighs, shakes her head.
```

If you really want to describe a camera movement, write the **experience** of it, not the technical term:

```
We slowly get closer to Jimmy.
```

not

```
SLOW DOLLY IN ON Jimmy
```

Don't Tell Them How To Do Their Jobs

Don't tell the actors how to act, the director how to direct, or the reader how to feel.

The exact facial expressions an actor will make, the set design or edits or visual style are simply not your decision. You certainly can try to convey a feeling by saying the character rolls their eyes or the light spills in from the kitchen...but be aware that the production will likely interpret those ideas in their own ways.

If you feel something will **only** work if they do it exactly a certain way, you are misunderstanding what a script is. It's a **plan**, from which all the other artists and craftspeople do their jobs.

Writing What Can't Be Filmed

Some people believe scripts should only contain what the camera can see or the microphone can hear -- because "they can't shoot what someone is thinking."

But the actor can **act** what they're thinking, and the director can shoot that.

It's part of your job to tell a story of feelings. If you can't write the inner state, you can end up trying to silent-movie it:

```
Jimmy picks up the clothes using just two
fingers, holding his nose with the other hand
and making a face like he's going to throw
up.
```

Isn't it just a lot better to write:

```
Jimmy picks up the clothes reluctantly, with
disgust.
```

Sometimes a quality of emotion is subtle or unspoken and you need to name them to help the actors, director and crew make those invisible, non-verbal things happen.

Keep these type of lines few and simple:

```
Addison suddenly regrets her decision.
```

-- seems like a nice touch, while

```
Jimmy is overflowing with class-conscious
contempt as he lets out a condescending
snort.
```

-- is less so.

Do be careful: writing things that can't be filmed **may** be a sign that you're not thinking in terms of dramatic action. I think the best advice is more of philosophy than a rule:

WRITE MOSTLY
what characters are saying or doing

SOMETIMES
what they think or feel

RARELY
how the filmmaking tells the story

Stylistic "Tricks" Are Completely Acceptable In A Script
Showy style is not a bad thing. It's fine to use:

<u>underline</u>

italics

bold

exclamation points!

random CAPITALIZATION

ellipses...

dashes---

But tricks get stale very quickly. Don't over-use them.

If you've been doing anything for a while, switch it up. If you have been writing very hype-y, talk plainly for a minute. If you have been slow and reasonable for a while, freak 'em out a little. And don't pile them up: only use one at a time.

Read A LOT of Scripts
And don't just read them. Analyze: try to figure out the mechanics, the tricks or tools, the approach. Look for things you can do, in your own way.

Pay attention to the writing style, the voice, the storytelling.

How do the writers you like use language?

Notice how different they can be. Don't try to look for the "best way" to write. Collect possibilities.

Work Out Your Style By Experimenting
Don't try to figure it out before you write -- learn by writing.

No one is tracking your style and holding you to it. While style probably should be consistent within a script, it can change from script to script.

Try out styles and tricks, see how they work, tinker with them to make them yours.

There is one absolute truth to remember, the one thing everyone in the business agrees upon about scripts:

**EVERYONE in The Industry
has TOO MANY scripts to read**

so they want your script to MOVE

They want you to do your job: create characters and story in dramatic actions.

The core of a script for a no-budget indie is the same as for a massive event movie:

**create the CHARACTERS
and tell their STORY**

**use your storytelling voice
to make it happen for the reader**

THE LESSON OF THE REACTION SHOT

A **reaction shot** is when you cut away from the action to someone in the story watching what's happening. This lets directors and editors change the pace of a scene or the order in which things happen.

(So, a note to aspiring directors: GET reaction shots!)

Take note when watching shows and movies of how often, during both physical action and dialogue, they cut away to the listener or to someone reacting.

Story-wise, it seems like a terrible idea. Doesn't it pull us away from the action?

Strangely, no: reaction shots have a powerful emotional effect.

the audience feels things in a more meaningful way when they see the effect on someone in the story

If you want us to feel a character is scary, have them scare someone in the story. If you want a character to be powerful, see them exerting power over other characters.

The reaction shot tells us that if you only think about the emotions of the hero and the villain, you write a shallow, simplistic story. The more you can put yourself and the audience into the feelings of **all** of the characters, the more complex and rich your story will be.

If you want the audience to feel anything other than the most simple emotions, you likely will have to engage them with multiple characters who each have a legitimate need or want, but whose needs are in conflict.

Think about what you want the audience to feel. Ask yourself: who, in the story, is feeling it?

Also, interestingly: we in the audience can strongly feel something that a character is **trying not to feel** (for example, holding back tears.) In that situation, it really helps if **someone** in the story is understanding, fearing, hoping for them.

So what we can learn as writers from the reaction shot?

DO NOT write "reaction shot of character x" into your script

DO make sure other characters are affected by events and involved in the fate and feelings of your main characters

You don't **always** need to have someone reacting. It's just a principle:

stories are about relationships

scenes are about interactions between people

the more all of those people feel, the better

DELIVER THE MOMENT

In *Monster*, John Gregory Dunne's unhappy memoir of working as a Hollywood screenwriter at the end of the 20th century, he dwells on a note he got repeatedly from the eminent-but-abusive producer Scott Rudin: "Deliver the moment."

On first reading, this just felt to me like a bit of sloganeering, the kind of phrase (like "raise the stakes") that non-writing people latch on to, suggesting an ethos of never-ending increase and perfectibility, a world of more.

But over time I found myself realizing it was good advice.

I think it's sort of a variation on the image Sidney Lumet used to describe the work of a director: making a mosaic -- selecting and polishing each individual bit of tile.

> **make each bit distinctive**
> **make us feel it**
> **make it matter**

This is an easy thing to forget in the frantic piling-up of moments that make a script. You begin to prioritize some. You create moments that are just a bridge between two other scenes. Or, having structured a moment to be decisive, you feel like the work is done and neglect to make it as rich and unique as you can.

Every scene has a distinctive action and feeling; be sure you identify it and do everything you can to heighten it, make it clear, make it effective.

what is the kick of this scene, the point, the feeling?

what is the style, the texture?

can I make it funnier -- or sadder, or faster, or smarter?

how can this moment be different from all the others?

how can it be as much as possible of what it needs to be?

Deliver the moment. Yes, it's an annoying slogan. But it's also true.

"BEATS"

"Beat" is a filmmaking term that can refer to several different things. Among the possibilities:

A Small Pause

In dialogue, "beat" is often a "parenthetical" (see "Script Format"), describing a little pause, a shift in tone or topic, or even just dropped in for rhythm or emphasis.

```
                    JOE
          You never liked me, did you?
          You took advantage of my
          connections but you don't
          respect me.
            (beat)
          You're a leech and you have
          bad taste in shoes.
```

A Scene

Some people refer to an outline as a "beat sheet," in which case each scene might be seen as a beat.

An Adjustment Or Change Within A Scene

Some people use "beat" to refer to "adjustments," signifying that a character is changing to a different action during a scene. In this case, it refers to steps or stages **within** a scene.

You generally have figure out what "beat" means by the context.

THE MAJOR MOVES

Sometimes when I'm thinking about the structure of a story, I divide it into sections: not quite acts, nor scenes, just "big hunks of story" tied together by something -- a mood or type of action, a problem, a sub-section of plot, a location or a time.

I call them "major moves." (The name is inspired by a line from Richard Price's script for *The Color Of Money*: "I'm a student of human moves.")

There are no rules for defining a major move: it's just a feeling.

They often begin or end with a set piece, a big discovery or revelation, a substantial change.

It's a way to get the shape of a story into your head, to feel the emotional shifts, to keep it from being a steady grind or too much of the same thing.

Often I will make a document that lists the major moves, just for myself.

SOME COMMON CAUSES OF BAD SCRIPTS

passive central character

unconvincing or missing character arcs

lack of cause-and-effect

repetition of action

lack of tension in scenes

lack of tension between scenes

dialogue that isn't action

dialogue lacks subtext

changing or ignoring the internal logic (the "rules" of the story or world)

things not changing

stereotype and cliches

ENDINGS

Endings are hard.

The ending has to answer the driving questions of the story. It is the resolution, the release of tension.

It is also the final statement, the vision. It's your parting gift to the audience.

It has to be bigger, better, climactic, ultimate.

It has to sum everything up, and at the same time let it all go.

And an ending has to do all this in a way that feels inevitable, yet surprising.

So my message about endings is:

don't put off work on the ending until the end

Think about the ending all along the way. Try to choose -- at least in a vague, general way -- how you want the story to end, early on in your process of writing.

I personally don't feel I can write until I know the ending. It gives me the vibe, the vision. Choosing the ending is when I feel the work is defined, locked, meaningful.

You can, certainly, write a script without knowing the ending. Writing the story may be how you find it. When you work that way, you may have to go back later to change things that steered in the wrong direction, or to lay in stuff that you only now realize you needed. That's fine, it's what rewriting is for.

There isn't a rule, formula or right way to work out your ending.

You have to decide what matters most to you.

These are some things to keep in mind as you do:

Resolve The Story
Make a choice, tell us what happens to end the suspense that has been driving us through every scene. Has the main character found a way to get what they wanted at the beginning? Have they conclusively failed to get it? What caused either of those two paths? How do we see it? What have we learned, or felt, or been provoked to think?

Release The Audience
Tell them it's over. Make clear that it's the end.

You usually need a decisive line, image, event. Often you refer to or use something from earlier in the story.

There are movie cliches to indicate the ending -- for example, the crane shot rising up, the fade out, the hard cut to black. You might write those -- but the really important job is crafting the action, the moment or the line **right before that**.

Maybe they'll fade out or maybe they won't, but the clear emotional insight, the invention and idea of that last beat -- that's what matters.

Ambiguous Endings
An ambiguous ending usually needs to be **definitively** ambiguous -- to clearly say to the audience: *we are not going to tell you more -- this is something for you to think about.*

(This is very different from a "cliffhanger" -- which tells the audience: *there is more to come.* In a very real sense, a cliffhanger is not an ending at all: the story is not over, we have simply come to the end of an installment or part.)

In general, the mainstream entertainment business is uncomfortable with ambiguity. It usually helps support this kind of ending if the story as a whole has been somewhat daring or unconventional. Uncertainty itself is often a key element or theme of stories with ambiguous endings.

The Coda

A scene or sequence after the climax and resolution of the story can be called a "coda."

Ideally these moments should be more than just a "tidying up" or a victory lap. They might show how the characters are handling the changes brought about by the ending, or steer our feelings about what happened. They might hint at forgiveness or new hopes, lasting damage or tragic lessons, reflections on all that went before or savoring a triumph.

Whatever you do in a coda, it should add to or shape our understanding of the people and the story. It tells the audience how to remember this story.

ANY SCRIPT IS A COMBINATION OF

A Hook, A Spark
something you thought was interesting, original
or powerful

Formula
from the genre and The Industry

Stolen Materials
all that stuff you love or hate or learned from

The "Zeitgeist" (Spirit Of The Time)
the culture you live in:
your world and historical moment,
whether you fit into it or not

Production & Collaboration
suggestions (or forced changes) from
producers, executives, directors, actors
plus everything that production brings,
from casting and financing to budget and locations

You
your instincts, feelings, preferences, experiences,
vision, style

THE
BALANCES

THE IDEA OF BALANCES

Some elements of writing only seem to exist in relation to each other.

You can't "solve" these oppositions. No matter how supremely committed you are to one side or the other, you'll never eliminate the push-and-pull between them.

I personally think this impure, unsettled quality is what makes art feel alive and magical -- because it's also the experience of life. Your efforts to balance these elements in each project is what breaks down formula and brings a texture of truth into your work.

Balances help you write in a very simple way:

**if something in a balance
isn't working:
think about the other side**

While an ideal balance should theoretically be in the exact middle, you will rarely find yourself there. With some you work like a pendulum, attending alternately to one concern or the other. Others require you to accept how much each side needs the other.

What follows is not a comprehensive survey. I'm sure there are more, and maybe some things are particular "balances" **for you**. I just want to get you started thinking this way.

PERSIST / LET GO

Most creative work does not get done without a stubborn, even delusional, refusal to quit. Sometimes grinding is necessary -- but it can also become a time-wasting trap. You need to know when to walk away, let it go.

When Should You Persist?
at least **part** of the process or the work itself is good or satisfying.

you notice a pattern of quitting, or you've never stuck it out

you are making progress, even if slow

your desire to quit is **only** based on the feeling that the work is bad or will fail

you are learning as you work

you're pretty new at this, and the process itself is new

When Should You Let It Go And Move On To The Next Thing?
you are not making any progress, despite trying many different approaches

if you are doing it only for someone else, or for some principle

there's absolutely no joy or satisfaction over a long period of time

the idea of quitting brings enormous relief and freedom and you are eager to try a new project

things have changed while you were working

it is causing you harm

Because this one is "either/or" -- you can't do both -- you're looking to balance the trend.

Ask yourself: **overall, am I persisting or giving up a lot?**

It is never going to be easy to make this choice.

It is heartbreaking to let something go: mourn it.

And you may not know which was right until you try one path and see what happens -- **so DO NOT throw the incomplete work away!** Make sure you can come back to it some other time if you want.

And if you decide to persist: take small steps, over time. Don't add pressure, maybe shift how you do the work or try something new within it.

CREATING / SHAPING

There are two kinds of writing: **creating** and **shaping.** They use different kinds of energy and likely come from different parts of the brain.

It might seem like there's a hierarchy, but they are each a form of creativity and either, alone, will not make a work of art.

(So, yes -- naming one "creating" probably isn't quite fair.)

Creating
means you spew out a magical mess. It requires an open frame of mind, a kind of trance. You are daydreaming, following impulse and instinct.

You must be willing to guess, to go wrong or too far, to not judge yourself.

Sometimes it comes out great, but mostly it doesn't. That's all right, though, because then you do the...

Shaping
is when you rework or rethink the mess -- using theory, analysis, taste. You refine, revise, make it better.

This requires you to judge and estimate, to be somewhat calculating or even formulaic. You are conscious of the mechanics, the plan, the goals, the choices.

The key to this balance: when you're doing one -- don't worry about the other.

You don't really work in the middle, they can't be done at the same time. The process of going back and forth between them is what makes writing good.

People think it's two chronological steps, but it's actually a constant back-and-forth -- sometimes so fast you don't even realize it.

You want to get so comfortable with this pattern that it doesn't feel like "failing and fixing," it feels like **working.**

Because it is.

FEELING / CRAFT

There are times you ride a river of divine dictation, in which a muse -- or your subconscious or the work itself -- is feeding you words and ideas. Other times you're chopping away at a block of granite with a screwdriver made for eyeglass-hinges.

Craft

is the mechanical, practical knowledge involved in an art. It may include mastering materials, tools, skills, methods, theory or history.

Craft helps you solve problems. It means you won't try to build a bridge out of balsa wood or a balloon out of iron. You spend less time reinventing wheels.

Craft makes it more likely for feeling to show up, and makes you more capable of taking advantage when it does.

It can make a safe place for feeling -- the way a nuclear reactor or steam engine contain the useful but volatile elements for their work.

Craft keeps you working when you don't feel like it.

Being able to provide craft on demand is a vital part of having a professional career.

But craft isn't enough.

I won't pretend there isn't plenty of successful empty craft out there, but to me -- without feeling, craft is hollow and mechanical.

Feeling

is the part of the work that comes from places you can't control or really understand. Call it talent or inspiration or magic.

Feeling is unique and individual -- but also the intangible subjective stuff that gets **shared** in art.

It is powerful, we hunger for it. It connects people, and makes art one of the best ways to get access to our own -- and each others' -- souls.

Feeling can steer craft, and give you a reason to make craft choices.

And it can motivate you to put up with the demands of craft, to do the work of learning and mastering it.

But following feeling can take you off cliffs and into dead ends. It's inconsistent, unruly and unreliable.

Also, the feelings you dig into for your work can be tied to personal problems or vulnerabilities -- which can derail, confuse or make the work painful.

If there was ever a balance where checking the other side can save your life, it's this one.

craft gives you a way to prompt and steer feeling

feeling gives you a reason to use your craft

FORM / CONTENT

Form -- structure, style, mechanics -- is a container, a delivery vehicle. It can't exist without content to deliver.

But content -- feelings and thoughts, characters and events -- are impossible to convey without form.

Any work of art goes from **abstract to concrete to abstract:** from one person's experience in their head -- to an object or performance -- to another person's experience in their head.

Mastering art is very much a matter of learning how to get comfortable with translating back and forth between form and content, abstract and concrete -- and accepting that you can't really predict or control the result of those translations.

When you write the word "purple," the color you imagine will never be exactly the "purple" in the mind of the reader or viewer.

It is magic, miraculous, that it happens at all.

The practical use: recognize the interdependence.

Putting too much emphasis on either side tends to make for bad art.

**if what you are working on is abstract (content) --
what do you need to do to make it concrete?**

**if what you are working on is concrete (form)
what abstract thing the audience will take from it?**

ESCAPE / ENGAGE

Do we use stories to escape from our lives, or to engage with the world?

The power of escape is obvious: we forget our troubles. We spend time in a world where things make sense. We get to imagine being romantic, amusing, athletic, heroic, ruthless, violent, graceful, wealthy or surviving an apocalypse.

But we also want stories to teach us or change us, to call out virtues and vices, explain history and examine society. Seeing things in a story makes them "real" in a way that information often doesn't. When you become absorbed in a story, you are living in another person's life -- feeling empathy and finding shared humanity.

It's important to remember that escape and engagement need each other.

Escape doesn't work if it doesn't engage, if there isn't some hook into real human relationships or emotions.

Further, escapist art still reflects the world -- through symbolic versions of real social, political, religious or historical situations; by exaggerating reality; or by exploring "what-if" alternatives. Whether they intend to be or not, no matter how fanciful (turtles and rabbits having races...) stories are about our lives.

At the same time, reality-engaged art needs the escapist pleasures of storytelling to convey its ideas and drive its emotions.

And turning life into a story simplifies reality, distorts it, gives it an unrealistic order and imposes meaning. No matter how topical or well-researched, stories will always be somewhat false and fanciful.

Escape/Engage is particularly complex in screen work because the art form seems to be a truthful recording of a real thing. But even without computer-generated graphics, artifice and illusion are built in: the frame, the lens, the edit all tamper with reality.

But this "lie" may be the best way to convey truths. We may not be able to handle the light outside our cave, but the projections on the wall help.

There is no way to avoid using both of these elements in any work. We need to escape reality in art; we use art to know and feel our reality.

I think the secret to this balance is:

**we will always escape and always engage,
in every story**

...so provide both

VISUAL / VERBAL

This has, sadly, become a polarized balance.

During the "Golden Age" of Hollywood (1920s-1960s), the difficulty of recording sound and the studio "factory system" made most screen stories stage-y and talk-y. Then technological change, the breakdown of studio control and the rise of film schools/film studies created a revolution that opened up screen language...but unfortunately also created a straw man enemy for "pure cinema" to vanquish: dialogue. "Film is a visual medium," became a war cry.

It is indeed -- but also a dramatic and narrative medium. "Pure cinema" does not exist. Screen storytelling is a unique and remarkable art because it combines so many others: drama, poetry, acting, painting, photography, music, costumes, props, sound, graphic arts, editing. To prioritize any one of them is to miss the power of the form.

But a script is only verbal

So screenwriters must perform a balancing act: using words to make imaginary movies -- while recognizing that we are only a part of the process.

The secret to this balance is letting go without giving up. Love the complex art of screen stories, and try to find words for it.

**embrace the haiku-like grace of screenwriting,
describe as simply and poetically as you can**

**think about what is essential
in a physical act, an atmosphere, a visual element,
not the detail or surface**

steer the reader to the emotional impact of the action

indulge in language, get good at using words

invoke, indicate, suggest, inspire

INFORMATION / SENSATION

Screen stories are made of stuff that stimulates our brains: color, motion, rhythm, sound, performance. Eye-candy, ear-candy, feeling-candy. This crude element of kicks should not be taken lightly. It's powerful.

But without a narrative, pure screen sensation can get confusing and numbing.

At the same time, screen stories convey a non-stop flow of information in those same images, sound and performance. Narrative and meaning both require information. The audience wants to know who people are and what they are doing.

But alas, information rarely offers up any sensation. It's just dull.

Sensation and information are both "baked in" to the experience of screen stories -- but neither gives a damn about the other. They make no room for each other, they have their own concerns.

So it is the artist's job to balance them.

It works out to a pretty simple mantra:

make sensation meaningful
&
information sensational

ARTIST / AUDIENCE

There are two versions of this:

> balancing the artist and audience within you

> balancing pleasing yourself with pleasing others

The Artist & Audience Within

To imagine the movie you want to write, you need to be its first audience.

But when you're doing the work, you also need to think like an artist. The pleasures of solving a puzzle or taking a ride are different from those of laying out clues or building tracks. Luckily, there is a real joy in the craft, the mechanics.

Even when the work is done, it's difficult to be your own audience. You see all the original dreams and influences, the wrong turns and phantom limbs.

Artists have to get used to being somewhat alienated from "normal life" in this way.

A work of art can take months or years of the artist's life. It has more meaning to the artist, they have more riding on it. For an audience, even the greatest artwork is just one of many.

But without keeping some connection to the audience and "normal life," an artist's work can become arcane and inaccessible.

I think this balance works by getting comfortable with living in two worlds at once -- thinking and feeling as both craftsman and enchanted user of the crafted work -- insider and outsider, never being whole...but maybe being richer for that complicated constant dance.

Pleasing Yourself Vs Pleasing Others

Acclaim and popularity are among the main ways we define success in art. Plus screen work is collaborative, so you **have** to please others.

And many artists have to get used to giving themselves permission to please themselves. It just sounds bad, arrogant, selfish.

So "please others" can weigh heavily, pulling this balance in one direction.

But if all you do is seek to fit into someone else's values, your work is unlikely to be good. If you worry about "losing" every possible audience member, you make something bland and worthless.

The audience wants the artist's vision.

Try to create a process and a style that makes room for both needs.

Be aware when you lean hard toward one side or the other. Be prepared for the likely consequences of either impulse, be ready to live with them.

The most distinctive element of this balance is: you can only truly control one side of it. You can never really know what will please others.

It is important to care about the audience. It is good for your art to try to see it through others' eyes. But in the end, you can't know what will "work" for them until it is too late.

So you make your best guess, balance these as best you can... and roll the dice.

If you feel a particular struggle between what you want to do and what you think others want you to do -- it can help to choose a goal for each project: to decide at the beginning when you begin whether you will be tilting to one side of the other.

Some people call this "one for them and one for me" but there's no actual reason to insist it be one-for-one. Even that is a balance.

ART / BUSINESS

The push-and-pull between art and business is hardly a secret
-- but until you're working in the "art business," it's hard to
grasp how intense this love-hate relationship is.

(Especially because -- at least lately -- most people in both fields
are desperately trying to deny they are in opposition.)

Alas, it is not simply that good art is bad business, or good
business is bad art.

It's easy to think that art is noble and refined, while business is
ruthless and crude. But art can be a shallow, self-indulgent drug
and business can be an honest attempt to reach more people,
give them delight or make their lives better.

If you're an artist, the dream is to make your living from art,
selling your pure work to an eager market. But in reality, most
money for art comes from "art jobs" -- using your skills and
talent for some business that has concerns other than your
work.

(Patronage -- support from a patron who likes art or likes
being seen as supporting art -- is almost impossible to find for
screenwriting, since it is an art that doesn't exist in a finished
form by itself, an art without an audience.)

Almost every form of distribution or exhibition to reach an
audience is a business. If you choose to distribute your own
work, you don't avoid that -- you just get in conflict with the
business part of yourself.

So: artists need business.

And unfortunately for the art business, it needs artists. They make the art. It must be immensely frustrating to have your business depend on unreliable, unpredictable and un-businesslike artists.

Worse, even when the artists are gung-ho to please business... art is subjective, personal and culturally determined. Despite endless efforts to find one, art does not have a formula or set of rules. Art is a mystery, and a gamble. Applying business metrics of value -- more popular, more sales -- rarely make great art.

Alas: that does not mean the "reverse formula" works: "Fine – I'll just write everything I hate (or everything business likes), and that'll make a million dollars." It doesn't work that way.

The end result: art and business are hopelessly tied to each other, and forever wishing they could be free.

The only way to handle this balance: understand the realities of both.

And then make choices. Recognize that every choice has a price.

ART / LIFE

This is a balance about being an artist, not about art.

if you make art, you step out of life,
but life is the source of art

life interferes with art,
art trivializes life

A writer's work is collecting and transforming life. We often work out our feelings or thoughts by writing about them. But we feel conflicted about revealing ourselves or using our experiences. It makes us vulnerable. We don't (or do!) want to hurt or offend.

Art -- making it or consuming it -- can ease our suffering and make our lives better. But you still have to engage in and work on your relationships, health, fears and finances. Your art can't actually fix your life.

All any artist can do is be conscious of the need to weigh desires and consequences. There's no right answer or way to handle this. It requires a non-stop balancing of many needs.

Each side of this balance enriches the other -- if we can learn to live with the way that each feels like it's taking away from the other.

Don't neglect your life for your work.

Don't allow your life to undermine your work.

This will be difficult. It will require you to be strong, to juggle, to negotiate and communicate, to sacrifice.

Be aware, be practical, be flexible.

life problems need life solutions

art problems need art solutions

BEING
A
WRITER

INSTINCT

Every time I try to explain how you make art, I keep finding myself wrestling with the same somewhat uncomfortable fact:

**creative work HAS to be
PERSONAL
& somewhat IRRATIONAL**

The **most important** basic operating principle for **every** artist is --

"I think this (particular thing) is good."
or
"this (particular thing) seems interesting"
or just
"I like this (particular thing)"

When you get too systematic or businesslike or theoretical, when you look away from yourself too much -- you take the art out of it.

The first time I thought about this, I was looking at a "continuous-line" drawing by Picasso. He did many of these, in which he would create a face, a bull or a bird from a single flowing line, without lifting the pen from the paper.

I was wondering: *how did he know the line would come out exactly like that?*

And I suddenly realized: **he didn't.**

He had faith in the gesture. In the **process.** All he **knew** was that it would be **his** line, in **that moment**...and that would be all right.

I spend a lot of time here talking about the mechanics of art and I do believe an artist does have to be a mechanic in many ways. But that's the form, the "body." There's something else operating, as well: the "spirit."

Call it talent or vision -- it's the part where we do things *"because I said so."*

People in The Industry don't like to talk about this, because it means the whole business is irrational and unpredictable (which is, unfortunately, the truth.)

And just in general, the vital importance of instinct is sort of an icky thing to declare -- because a romanticized vision of the "impulsive genius" can just bring out the worst in people, so an essential fact about making art got tangled up with excuses for bad behavior.

To do creative work, you need to be in touch with your thoughts and feelings -- your irrational, embarrassing, vulnerable inner stuff.

This does not mean that anything goes and nothing matters.

**a lot of the work of being an artist
is learning how to trust & work from
your feelings & instincts
without becoming
a destructive asshole**

Instinct isn't everything. It's not the end of the process. It's what you apply all that skill and theory and craft to.

An artist has to learn how to be irrational in a systematic, mechanical way -- and how to survive being emotional, self-centered and irrational as part of their work routine.

So let's talk about how you get comfortable with, and competent at, making instinctive choices.

Recognize That Instinct Is A Necessary Part Of The Work
This is not something you're imposing on otherwise reasonable system.

It's **required.**

Accept that your choices will come from a wide variety of places inside yourself.

memories

fears

feelings

experiences

beliefs & theories

all the stuff you've loved -- or hated

That messy pile of raw material is where you should go to get stuff to work with.

Give yourself permission. Consciously follow your impulses. When you have to make a choice and find yourself struggling, or when you can't think of what to do -- try thinking: maybe the solution here is just **whatever I decide it is.**

Learn To Listen To Yourself
We are taught all our lives to be rational and reasonable and **not** operate from our feelings. Feelings are scary, they can be selfish, they can go out of control, they make people uncomfortable.

So listening to them is **not easy.** It's something most of us have to work at.

Practice
It takes time to get comfortable doing this. You will feel self-conscious. You will not always **know** what you want. You will ask: is that **really** my instinct? Is it my **best** instinct?

It's not just the first thing that pops into your head.

It takes practice to recognize the **feeling** of creative choice. And there really is no other way to describe it: it's just a feeling that one thing is sometimes just a **little more right** than anything else.

So practice. Listen to your feelings, let your impulses talk to you. Sometimes it'll work, sometimes it won't. Just keep trying it, over time.

Identify The Source Of Negative Voices In Your Head
If you are thinking: *this is bad, this might fail, you're blowing it...* you are **not** actually working.

Stop and ask where that voice is coming from.

is it an expression of something you fear?

someone you think you have to please?

who is judging you? How real is that?

I have never heard of a single moment when creativity was negative.

Those other voices are not always wrong -- but they only help **after** you have been positive, instinctive, creative.

I don't mean you have to create cheerful, uplifting stuff. Your work can be mean and angry and upsetting. But when you're working on that dark scary stuff, you will still feel: *oh, cool - maybe this - or try this - oh this is better - yeah, that's fun.*

Those other voices are not always wrong -- but they only help **after** you have been positive, instinctive, creative.

Lower The Pressure
Work on following your instincts when you have time and privacy to make a mess. Do it when no one is looking but you.

And even if you instinctively make messy or even bad art: what's the worst that can happen? Somebody might not love it. Who cares? Get used to that, its part of the game.

Trusting Your Instincts Does Not Mean ONLY Listening To Yourself
Screenwriting is a collaborative profession. You do actually have to get good at following rules, taking notes and doing what you're told.

I personally believe when you get good at the inner voice, truly confident that **you'll** be there for you...then you can more easily hear what others say.

There's a simple test for whether you're being a defensive jerk: *do you **ever** agree with a criticism*? If everyone else is wrong all the time...that's your problem.

(And by the way: if you feel like everyone else is **right** all the time -- sooner or later your head will explode because people will always have opinions and they will never all agree.)

Get Good Enough To Make Your Instincts Work
You have to be practical, hard-working, determined and strong. Develop your skills and process.

Instinct and feeling are a source of power, but you still need a working machine to turn that energy into something useful or valuable.

Be Willing To Fail

So often when we go against our instincts, it's because we are trying to avoid the possibility of pain and failure.

But is it impossible to avoid creative failure. Things are not going to go as you hope or imagine. Even when they go right, it will rarely be as you hope or imagine. Living with that is part of being an artist.

Working from your instincts means you have to own the good, the bad and the ugly. You have to say *"yep - that is what it is, and I did it."*

The best way to do that is to make choices you can live with, even if they fail.

Learning to create from your instincts is not necessarily a path to success.

But as far as I can tell: it's your best shot.

Your work will succeed in some ways and fail in others -- and none of it will be entirely what you expect.

All you can know for sure is that it will be **your** line, in **that moment**...and that will be all right.

TALENT

Talent is: a natural ability to do something. And, yes: some of us seem to have more, or less.

But it's not that simple.

there are a lot of DIFFERENT talents
at work in any art

For example, these are just **some** of the abilities that help a writer:

structure a story

write dialogue

empathize with characters

be funny

(or scary or romantic etc...)

put things into cause-and-effect sequence

set-up and pay-off

withhold and reveal information

use language well

work in a certain genre

create original work

make choices

make connections

summarize

remove the repetitive or extraneous

write quickly

discipline yourself to write

make changes easily

critique yourself

hear criticism productively

pursue a vision

put your craft in the service of others

communicate & collaborate about the work

No one has **all** of the "component talents" -- and **none** of them are make-or-break.

Everyone has strengths, gifts, natural abilities. Some are recognized and rewarded more than others, but **all of them** are actually valuable.

the real question is:
what are you going to DO
with the GIFTS YOU HAVE?

I think dealing with that question breaks down to 4 steps:

Figure Out Which Talents You Have

Study your art: not finished artworks but the process, the work, the job.

Ask: what are the talents involved in doing this thing?

Then you have to learn which you are naturally good at. Make judging your own work, and way of working, part of your process. "Judge" does not mean condemn or criticize -- it means **honestly know yourself.**

(If you believe you're good at everything -- or at nothing -- think again.)

There is no absolute test or marker for talent. Many magnificent artists were told early on that they were worthless. Unfortunately, that does not mean being told you are worthless is a marker for talent. It's all just very complicated.

Talents are not always easily visible. They may be buried or undeveloped -- or the person looking has never done the work and doesn't really understand what talent is.

So here are just **some** things to look for, as you try to figure yourself out:

At Least Part Of The Work Comes EASILY
Figure out which parts of the art process come easily or energize you. **Something** in there will feel right, good, natural.

But since "what feels good" can get muddied up by doubt and fear, also consider if you feel:

Pleasure In Doing The Work
It's not always fun, of course. It can be stressful misery. But **even then**, most artists feel **some** kind of a "yes" when they work on their art. Even when you're failing or incompetent (which we **all** are, often) it feels in some way interesting, engaging, right, real, worthwhile.

Try to break down what feels good: what aspect of it, exactly, do you **like doing**?

Love Of The Mechanics

You have a fascination with how people do this thing, the inner workings, the nuts & bolts -- the process. You want to know about it, and be around people who are into it.

Willingness To Engage Your Feelings

I can't really think of any example of talent that doesn't involve the artist engaging personally with the form or the content.

Persistence And Determination

Art requires real, somewhat insane, persistence. You have to need to do it enough to put up with the struggle, uncertainty and emotional turmoil.

You have to plunge in and try, **without knowing** if it will be good.

Talented people mess up -- a lot. But they try again, all sorts of different ways.

The desire to keep learning and growing is a sign of talent.

People Will Tell You

It is hard to get praise when you're starting out. Most "civilians" can't see past inexperience and lack of polish, and people in The Industry often "help" by telling you what's wrong with your work.

So learn to accept even partial, limited, backhanded praise. Take your wins where you can get them. Ask yourself:

did they follow the story?

did they get the idea or the feeling?

did **any part** of it work?

If what you do is getting **some** kind of positive response: take that seriously.

Figure Out What Your Talents Get You

Talent is not always rewarded. Often talent puts you into conflict with business, and sometimes it makes you hard to work with.

You may have talents that don't pay. Many don't. You may be gifted at an art with a small audience. It doesn't mean that isn't a talent, it means:

**you have to FIGURE OUT
how you are going to
MAKE A SUSTAINABLE LIFE
while you do your art
(like EVERY artist)**

Every artist, seriously. It never stops.

Work On Developing Your Talents

Talents don't just work by themselves. You have to work at them.

Gather experience and skills. Study and practice the craft.

Experiment, explore. Put in the time.

Learn what to do with your talent, how to let it guide you – and how to steer it.

Work On Building Up Or Replacing
What You Don't Have Talent At

Talent is a natural ability, it makes the work easier -- but even if it's not easy, you can still do it.

talent can be compensated-for with
skills
tools
study
practice

If you don't have a gift, you can at least put together a set of workable techniques or principles to follow -- and practice those skills for 10,000 hours.

YOU HAVE SOME TALENT
what matters is WHAT YOU DO WITH IT

figure out the talents you have

figure out what they get you

work on developing and using your talent

work on building up what you don't have talent at

CONFIDENCE

When you write a sentence or a story, you are taking a risk, leaping into the unknown. This requires a kind of bizarre faith -- or delusion -- that it's going to work out well.

How do you get that?

Most people, especially struggling artists, get it backwards: they think success will give them confidence.

But many successful people have talked about dealing with a paralyzing loss of confidence **after** becoming successful -- and how, in fact, success often gave them a sense of **additional** pressure and fear.

The truth: confidence or lack thereof has very little to do with how "good" or "bad" you actually are (whatever the hell those words even mean.)

Mostly:

confidence is something
you BRING TO the work,
not something you GET FROM it

You can't hype yourself into it. You can't force yourself to feel it. Some people seem to be simply (and often incorrectly) born with it, but most of us have to **build** confidence -- with **experience.**

I believe:

confidence = NOT being AFRAID

Even if you struggle (as I do!) with a brain chemistry chock full of the stuff that makes you fight-flight-or-freeze -- the more you **do** a thing, the more you experience it, the more confidence you have.

You build confidence by doing four things:

Practice
You do complex things every day that require a lot of confidence, without realizing -- because you don't remember how hard it was to learn to walk or talk.

You got to that level of skill by practice.

An athlete or musician is expected to practice until they they know how to do it without even thinking. A writer should do the same thing.

Get Experience
You can't **study** experience. You have to experience it.

Build your experience in low-stakes, "small time" circumstances. If you were playing a sport you wouldn't start at the championship, you'd start at some dinky local match.

So write some things just because you can **get them done**: a handmade zine, a web short, an open-mic night, your school literary magazine, putting on a show in your backyard.

You will fail. That's how you learn. You cannot avoid or skip the parts where you fail.

...but that will be all right, if you:

Focus On The Work
Don't work toward a result beyond the craft, the contents, the

qualities of the work itself. Work on whatever specific creative challenges you're trying to accomplish.

Confidence goes kablooey when you think about things outside the work: some judge or contest or reward. Those things actually have nothing to do with you. They are not **in** the work -- so why are you working on them?

Focus On The Fun
Have fun -- **enjoy** it. The artist's joy is part of how they make something great.

Does this mean having fun is an indicator of great work? Alas, no. There's plenty of awful stuff out there where the creators had a blast, and many great works came from a process drenched in misery. Creative work can be hard, painful and frightening.

But I believe even within all that legendary artistic suffering, there were moments of joy.

The joy is in solving problems, making discoveries, making progress and just...creating stuff.

One last trick I want to share about confidence. It's a really important one:

act as if you have faith
and you will be given faith

Also known as:

fake it 'til you make it

Do the thing you want to do, **even though** you don't believe it will be good.

Do it badly, do it the best you can -- because this is the real truth of creative confidence:

**the BEST kind of confidence is not
being sure you will win**

it's not really CARING if you win or lose

because you LIKE DOING THE THING

Win or lose, you're playing the game. It won't kill you and you'll play again, because that's who you are and that's what you do.

IMAGINATION

Louise Fitzhugh's novel *Harriet The Spy* begins with aspiring-writer Harriet showing her friend Sport how to do what she calls "playing Town":

She makes up a town, and figures out who lives there, as well as their jobs, relationships and personalities. Then she starts to make up stuff that happens to them one evening. There's a robbery at the local gas station while at the same time a baby is being born...

Harriet is making something up in her mind and getting lost in the reality of this thing that is not real.

This type of getting-lost-in-your-imagination is one of the most mythologized and misunderstood parts of creative writing.

I chose to describe this scene because (aside from the fact that I think *Harriet The Spy* is one of the great books of the 20th century): "playing Town" is a phenomenal insight into the pure pursuit of imagination.

Harriet's not talking about **doing** anything with "Town." She's not going to turn it **into** anything. She's just making stuff up because she likes making stuff up.

This perfectly dramatizes how all we do to capture or communicate what we imagine (i.e, art) is a very different thing from our imagination itself.

imagination is a PART of art
it's a SOURCE of art
but it is not art

And it is definitely not a career or a business: no one will pay you to do it.

Once you start to craft what you imagine for others, you're not playing Town any more.

a lot of becoming a good writer
is learning a practical method
for getting comfortable with
going back and forth
between imagination and craft

So what exactly **is** this "imagination" thing -- and why do we like it so much?

Even people with no feeling for or interest in art have this weird ability to create a fake reality and kind of **live in** the created moment.

In some ways I think it's a runaway variation on the survival skill of **making plans**: we figure out the consequences of things we might do by playing out an imaginary future.

But it's also a way we put ourselves in someone else's shoes. It may even be the source, or engine, of empathy.

Or do we simply use it to escape from reality? Which can be a really important thing to do in life.

Imagination is clearly related to dreams: another name for it is **day-dreaming.**

But Harriet's name for it points out that it is also a form of **play.**

I believe it's all of the above. I think those practical brain operations took on a life of their own, when our brains started saying: *I don't even care if it's a practical skill -- it's **fun**! I'm gonna keep doing it!*

The point: imagination is not just a tool to do some other thing.

It's a **basic part** of the human mind.

And that is really important because it means:

**your imagination
DOES NOT CARE
about your art**

So if you want to be an artist because you're a big "imagine-r" -- it's likely you're going to get into situations where your art and your imagination are in conflict.

Because when you write, you need to imagine. But then to craft something out of that experience, you often have to **betray** your imagination -- attending to the realities of the medium or business or community standards or working with other people.

And also because: imagination exists only in your mind -- and only in the moment. You can't save or share it. The exact sensations and emotions you have when imagining cannot be communicated.

When you try to do that, you turn it into another thing -- a picture or a script or whatever.

All this conflict between art and imagination often makes artists feel like they have (or are) messed up -- but I think it's just that you want to do two different things.

So a vital part of being a working artist is:

**accept that this process
(making art from imagination)
includes transforming the original impulse
into something else**

Instead of fighting that reality, you can start to look forward to the process of transforming magical kicks into artsy tricks.

When you accept that, and enjoy it: you start discovering the things that actually become the work.

And you begin to appreciate that it's kind of a miracle that **any** of this stuff connects at all.

I think that's one of the most exciting and profound things about art: when it works -- when something you crafted from your imagination thrills, inspires or amuses someone else, when somebody "gets" **any** of it, no matter how damaged and partial -- it's a unique satisfaction, in many ways more rewarding than money or praise.

It's **almost** as good as playing town.

So here are some tips on balancing art and imagination:

Recognize The Limits Of Imagination
You can't actually live there. It takes you out of the real world, where you need to be (most of the time) to take care of yourself.

It can get kind of addictive, in the negative sense of that word.

It can put you in conflict with your art, as previously noted.

It's finicky & unpredictable. It does not respond well to being organized or having to show up or being steered.

Enjoy The Power Of Imagination
It's yours. No one can stop you from using it. No one can take it away or tell it what to do.

It's a source of strength, because it doesn't care what anybody thinks.

It serves some vital purpose in our mind. They say your brain needs to dream at night; I think a lot of us need to imagine when awake.

Recognize The Independent Value Of Make-Believe
Let it be what it is. It doesn't always have to be art.

You eat or exercise or read a book without expecting to be paid or recognized for it. Maybe sometimes you should think of your imagination that way.

You'll feel less stress and conflict if you admit that sometimes what you really want is the unique escape of free imagination.

Figure Out The Place In Your Process For "Playing Town"
Know which one you're doing, when you're doing it. Be aware when you are "going there." Go there to discover and invent, to get emotional and creative power. Just don't expect it to obey the rules or the business.

The more you allow imagination to be what it is, the better it works.

If You're Going To Use Imagination For Art, Be Ready To Work With It
It's the gold you can make into a piece of jewelry -- if you're willing to melt it and bend it and only use as much as the piece requires.

Give some respect to this weird thing we do in our heads and stop expecting it to pay your rent or take over everyone else's head.

Sometimes you do stuff with it, and that's cool -- but sometimes you should just let yourself play.

MY FEAR OF WRITING

(This chapter tells you how I came to believe in the "lessons" on this topic. For ease of use, the lessons themselves have their own chapter.)

I started wanting to be a writer very young, about 11 years old. Books, movies, theater and art were my escape from crippling anxiety and existential horror. I was prolific and creative in high school: I made short films, painted, wrote a novel, a few plays, some radio plays and a screenplay. They were pretty good, for a kid.

But whenever I tried to write anything "serious" -- stories I wanted to submit to magazines, novels I wanted to send to publishers: I froze. I could only write scattered bits, or made plans for things that I never actually wrote.

I had a set of conditions which I felt would let me write something challenging or "serious": I had to have all day free, uninterrupted, with a pitcher of instant iced tea to drink and music playing. But even on those rare days when I could arrange all that, I would get lost or stuck.

I really didn't want to go college, but I gave it a year. All I kept thinking during that year was: *I have to be a professional writer, now.* As my second year began, I had a crisis. I felt there were too many demands on me. It was very clear that college was getting in the way of my being a writer.

Realistically: I was only taking four classes, of which two were literature and a third was playwriting. My homework was mostly just reading novels. I didn't care what grades I got, so academic pressure was low. I had a single room. Meals were right there in the dining hall.

College was, in other words, not getting in the way of anything.

But I couldn't make creative decisions. I couldn't choose the first line of a play. The moment was a man and a woman in a living room:

```
Do you want some wine?
Have a glass of wine?
Wine?
```

I could **not** decide which was right.

It didn't feel like fear.

It felt like something was getting in the way of writing. Everything was irritating and distracting. I agonized over it, then told my parents I wanted to quit school: I asked them to give me the money they were paying for college, so I could be a writer full-time.

They said no to that plan, but -- though they had just moved and my childhood bedroom was gone -- if I wanted to leave school to write, I could live in the spare room in their new basement.

I dropped out of college that October. It felt **urgent**. I absolutely had to solve this problem of becoming a professional writer, right away.

So: I was living in New York City, a cultural center. I had a supportive family, emotionally and financially. I was talented, determined, hardworking and privileged. I had all day free, with music to listen to and a typewriter -- the exact perfect conditions *I had set for writing. I had everything going for me.*

I could not write.

I like writing. It comes easy for me.

But as soon as I thought "this one is real, this one matters"...I froze up.

I needed to do something first -- read this book, buy that record, see this movie that's like what I'm writing, go for an inspiring walk. It felt like I was working on the wrong project, so I kept setting things aside and starting new ones.

By June, I was cracking up. It was suddenly very clear: I couldn't write in a basement.

I asked my parents to pay for a hotel room. I was going to bang out a first draft of a play in a few days. And (bless their hearts) they said okay. I packed up my typewriter and notes and went to a fairly nice hotel. I checked in, unpacked my typewriter....and realized I had lost my mind.

I couldn't write a play in three days. I couldn't write any better in a hotel room. This was a stupid, shameful writer's-block rock-bottom. I didn't write a word. I went home about an hour later.

I realized I had a problem. But I had no idea what to do about it.

Not long after, I got a clue: I was trying to write that play -- but instead, I imagined an opening sequence for a movie about the play's characters, set to the song I was listening to.

I wrote it -- easily. 6-7 pages. I knew it was good.

But the next day I couldn't go back to writing the play. Same old frozen, distracted problems.

The screenplay scene told me: **there IS a way out of this**. I just had to figure out what had happened in that writing session.

Was it because I was writing a screenplay, not a play? (Nope. Tried that.) Maybe it was the song I was listening to? (For God's sake, seriously?)

I decided to go back to college while I figured it out. I couldn't keep living in my parents basement, not-writing. At least in college I could look like I was making progress in life and avoid having to deal with real-life stuff like getting a job for the next three years.

Nine years later:

I had been working in various offices, mostly as a temp, for six years. I was determined to become a full time professional writer, so after college I refused to take any kind of "real" job. I worked in a different office every week, sometimes every day.

I worked on writing **every day.** I tried to write before work, at 4 or 5 in the morning, and then at other people's desks when there was a lull in the filing, copying and answering phones.

This was the exact opposite of my original need to have all day to write, uninterrupted. I got ten or fifteen minutes at a time, with no privacy, and I never knew when it would be.

Writing was still the same frustrating dance. I kept changing projects. I worked on notes and outlines, researched for months, read inspiring books and watched inspiring movies...but almost never finished anything I was writing.

I was at a temp job desk, and work was slow. I got my work-in-progress notebook (pre-laptops) out of my briefcase (pre-backpacks).

I was working on a novel. In the scene I was trying to write, the main character finds a dead body in his apartment. The phone is disconnected (pre-cellphones), so he runs out to call the police from the pay phone on the corner.

I focused on what happens in that one moment. *What does he say, what does it feel like?*

I mixed imagination and experience. I wanted him at a breaking point: I put him in my very real shoes, with folded cardboard in the bottom to cover the hole where the sole had worn through. I made it worse: I put him in a rainstorm. I described how his socks felt -- cold and squishy and humiliating.

He's trying to explain his bizarre situation to a skeptical cop on the phone. He is being forced to face the series of well-intended bad decisions that brought him to this moment. I thought about how reluctant he would be to tell it, which broke the dialogue up into a funny-awful series of baffled questions and awkward replies.

And I realized: THIS IS HOW YOU WRITE.

It had taken me 15 years to see it -- but when I did, it was as clear and stark as if illuminated by lightning.

You figure out the moment and you ask yourself questions. You write this one sentence, this one paragraph, to make this one moment happen in words.

No matter how much you think you should be doing something else, something first, something better. No matter how awful you know it's going to be.

Just this one moment, right now. Make it work. Just a sentence, a small step, a handful of words. Bring one thought, one scene, to life.

If you can do that, then you can do another one, and another.

All the other stuff -- the figuring it out and making it great --

can only happen if you do this, as much as you can.

All my life I'd been writing, when I did, by tricking myself. Switching projects, giving myself some inspiring challenge, riding the rush for a minute, trying to hype myself enough to forget the fear and stress.

I had to work that way because I had been putting enormous, ridiculous pressure on writing: it had to set me up with a full-time career, make me rich and famous. That was making it **incredibly hard** to write. I was completely gripped by fear every time I tried.

Instead, I had to learn how to make writing a comfortable, routine, enjoyable thing to do -- for myself, whether or it made money or not. I had to forget about all that other stuff and focus on the work itself, the pleasure of doing it.

This was **not** the end of my creative struggles. There were still years and years of those to come. But this was the tool that got me through each of them.

HOW TO DEAL WITH THE FEAR OF WRITING

It doesn't always feel like fear.

It might feel like you're simply "seeing" or "knowing" that you are not good enough -- or allowed -- to create. Or it might feel like you're realistically seeing a problem that you have to stop and solve...except you only stop, you never solve.

> **"The specific character of despair is precisely this: it is unaware of being despair."**
>
> **- Soren Kierkegaard**

Creative fear is like a filter over your mind: it won't let you see what you're doing, it takes away your enthusiasm and motivation, it throws off your judgement.

The most important thing to do about fear is **recognize** it -- to realize: *oh, this is that thing that happens to people's minds sometimes, where they get stuck under clouds and start to think that's the whole sky.*

That's why a lot of what helps is just **trying** stuff, **doing** stuff -- so you can stumble into a glimpse of the sky.

Fear is usually overcome by a mixture of understanding what it is and how it works, along with some kind of gradual process of confrontation with it.

See It For What It Is, And Slowly Get Familiar
Repeat small steps to make small advances in doing the thing you fear. Safe, limited exposure to accustom yourself, to

increase your tolerance.

Recognize The Pressure You Are Putting On Yourself

Adding pressure is almost never a good solution to creative problems.

Name Your Fear

It can help to face it, recognize it -- write it down, just for yourself:

> *this work is bad*
> *it won't sell*
> *I can't do it fast enough*
> *it's not worth it*
> *I'm not doing it like they say*

Then you can ask yourself: ***So what?***

Seriously -- worst case scenario: *what if this work is bad? If it* ***doesn't*** *sell? What's the* ***worst*** *that can happen?*

Is that worst thing really so terrible?

What the hell, even if you **are** actually, irredeemably awful: you might turn out to be another Ed Wood or Tommy Wiseau and your terrible-ness may stir a kind of joy.

That might sound flippant or sarcastic, but it's really the best advice I know when frozen by fear: *so what?*

If you like playing tennis, but you're never going to be a professional: would you not play tennis?

I suspect there are really just **3 creative fears:**

someone is going to judge you

it won't come out like it is in your head

you're not going to be what the world told us a writer
was: a celebrated person who pays
the rent by creating what they like

So I'm going to tell you the secret that defuses all of those fears:

EVERYTHING YOU FEAR AS A WRITER
IS GOING TO HAPPEN

everything you write WILL be judged

it will NEVER come out like it is in your head

almost NO writers make a full time living from writing,
and maybe one percent of professional screenwriters
get to write what they want,
the way they want

So what?

Now you can work, within all that..."failure."

The only way to get as good as you can, go as far as you can -- is
to **do it.**

No one can know, before they begin, how their creative work
or career is going to go. So your insistence that it has to go a
certain way is just...made-up. It's a fantasy.

ALMOST EVERYTHING WE FEAR CREATIVELY
is just the
LOSS OF AN IMAGINARY FUTURE

if you let go of that
you can create

No one can stop you from writing. You don't need permission or approval.

You started to write because somewhere inside, it was fun. It was interesting. It made some kind of emotional sense.

Then it is worth doing.

GETTING STUCK OR LOST

You can't write. You can't think. Your work, your life and basically **you***...all seem worthless. It's. The. Worst.*

And it is going to happen. It happens to **everyone.**

But every artist gets stuck or lost in their **own way.**

So you've got to get **past it** in your own way.

While creativity is unbelievably exciting -- it's also very unreliable and frustrating. Most artists get to a moment in which how-they-work doesn't work.

This is just a bunch of things to try. They won't all work for you, but some might.

In no particular order:

Remember: It's Just A Thing
First of all -- and this is **not easy** -- this thing you're writing: it's not your life, it's not your future, it's not a test. It doesn't decide or prove anything.

It's just a thing, in a world full of things.

If you feel like it matters **so much** that you're paralyzed with fear, you're expecting too much from your work. Back up a step, and...

Set Specific And Achievable Expectations
Think about accomplishing things like:

    telling a story people can follow

    provoking a feeling

    communicating an idea

Those might feel like they're not enough -- but they're more than you're doing right now.

Get Comfortable With Uncertainty

Creative work is stressful. Not-knowing how you're going to solve a problem or if the work will be any good stirs up very real doubt and fear. You have to plunge into that state over and over, pretty much every day.

Writing is a process of changes and discoveries. Learn to enjoy that.

Before you create something, you will have many, many questions. You can only answer them by creating it. You are figuring out the form and content of a thing which does not yet exist. It's simply not going to work exactly like you want or plan.

Get comfortable with saying:

> **I don't know yet, but I will**
> **-- because I am making choices,**
> **and with every choice I make,**
> **other choices become clear.**

Trust The Process

Create - revise - create - revise.

This is how it goes. This is how it **has** to go.

Learn How To Write Badly

The blank page is terrifying. Put **something** on it. Once there's a single word written down, the panic starts to ease.

Creativity needs something to cling to. Throw down absolute junk. It is not a waste of time. It will raise questions you never thought of.

Even the most crude notes are the dirt in which new ideas can grow.

One thing that helps me write total crap is knowing I'm going to feel really smart and competent when I look at it later and start to fix it.

If you can get used to writing badly, then you'll write.

Build On What's Good
Find **something** in the work that kind of pleases or entertains or interests you.

It doesn't even have to be actually good. It can just be something you **intend** to be good -- and then you can ask: *what can I do to make it a little better?*

Make Choices
Most people try to solve a script problem by throwing words at it. The real solution is to make choices.

Every choice conquers fear and defines your project a little bit more.

Narrow it down, define the choice. Then pick one path and see where it goes.

If you're trying to solve a problem and it's not getting solved, ask yourself:

> **what is the CHOICE that is making
> this step of the process difficult?**

Work With An Experimental Attitude
"Let's see what happens" is very different from *"Let's get this right."*

You aren't even sure yet what "right" is. Things change as you work. You learn and discover. Make some room for that.

Figure Out Where You Want To End Up

Try to invent or choose the end of the scene, the end of the story, the last thing they say in the conversation, the way the character will be when we see them later or last.

Name where you need to get, then you can start to figure out how you need to get there.

Figure Out What It's About

If I can't write something, often it's because I don't know what it's about. Even when I was sure I had it...I've had to stop and ask:

> what is the heart, the core of this scene (or character, or project)?
>
> what is the **main** thing I need to accomplish here?
>
> what is the most important purpose or message or kick?

Come up with a single answer. Not a big pile of things, not even two. There may be many things in your work, but choose one as the center.

Test Each Part

When a machine isn't working, sometimes you figure out what's wrong by methodically checking each part of it, one by one.

If you're stuck on something -- look at each element of the story around it, even the ones you are certain are okay: *is it the dialogue -- or this character -- or this event?*

You'd be surprised how often you find something that you didn't realize is no longer working. Often you can change it, or get rid of it, and boom! you're writing again.

Do One Thing At A Time
If you feel like **everything's** bad: the word "everything" is a sign that you're freaking out and should stop and just work on one task at a time.

Get In the Moment
Focus on what needs to be accomplished in just one moment of your story.

Just what the people are feeling and doing in that one moment.

Tell Yourself The Story
Write it down, scene by scene. Notice where it's easy to tell and where you get fouled up.

Return To The Inspiration
Think about what made you want to write this, remember something you love about it.

Use The Formula -- Or Toss The Formula
If you really can't believe in your project, choose a system: follow some book or teacher's plan and stick to it. Or just study the form or style of something you like and do **your** version of that.

But! If you are already working within a formula and you can't write...it may mean the formula is boxing you in. Try tossing it! Do what you want, even if the rules say it's "wrong."

Go Back To A Familiar Ritual
Sometimes it helps to do it like you did before: to follow a

pattern or habit that worked in the past, to make your process as familiar as possible so the only "moving part" is the work itself.

But if that isn't working -- try the opposite:

Change It Up
If what you're doing is not working: do **something** different.

If you work at home, go out to a coffee shop. If you are overthinking everything try writing without a plan. If you can't think of a line, think about the character. If a scene is stuck, work on another.

Stay flexible, try things. It's better than continuing to run head-first into the same wall.

Ask: What Am I Clinging To?
When you find yourself wrestling with pieces of a story that just don't fit together, it's usually a sign that you're clinging to some element.

It's hard to recognize what is jamming you up, because it **seems** necessary. When you begin to suspect you're clinging to something -- try to break the spell: see if you can do without it, or do it differently.

If it's really worth keeping, then you probably have to change or lose something else. That's cool -- either way: you're making a choice.

Ask: Who Am I Listening To?
When you're terribly stuck and it's really hard to write, sometimes that means you're putting someone else's values above your own.

Think about what you **think** you're doing wrong...and ask: is that really so awful? Why?

Whose voice is it, telling you that something isn't working, can't work, is bad?

Maybe you need to set that voice aside for a while. You can always check in with it later, but right now: it's getting in the way.

It's Not What You Imagined
Another frequent reason people can't write: the failure of what comes out to match what's in our mind.

We all use a vision of what it'll be like to inspire and steer toward -- but that can never be the art. This is a disappointing and scary fact, until you get used to it.

Learn to enjoy those moments when you meet the thing you're actually making, and start to work with it.

Art Problems Have Art Solutions
Your work problem may not be an art problem.

If you you keep having the same problem in different pieces of work -- that's likely not about a particular project's creative issues. It's about how you're doing it or thinking about it.

Work on the thing getting between you and the work: the feeling or fear or habit or belief.

Slow Down
This one might seem counter-intuitive, especially when you're stuck -- but a single sentence, an exchange of dialogue, five or six lines, might be a day's work. It might only take a half-hour.

That's okay.

The next day, another bit more. Another brick in the wall (in a good way.) Bit by bit, you get yourself through a bad patch.

Give Yourself Little Rewards
The pain is real. Comfort yourself. Make it absurdly transparent: *write a paragraph, give yourself a cookie.*

Step Away And Do Something Else
This kind of work, which looks like just sitting around, burns up serious brain energy. Take note if you're "fried" and set it aside.

Step away so you can step back. Do something else. Take your mind off it. Maybe just for ten minutes or maybe until tomorrow.

Live Your Life
Do not make your work your whole life.

    eat
    sleep
    exercise
    clean up
    talk to people
    amuse yourself

And then try again tomorrow -- because you can and you should.

GETTING NOTES

In writing for screens, criticism is called "notes."

The single most important thing you need to know about notes:

if THEY own the project:
FIND A WAY TO TAKE THE NOTE

if YOU own the project:
YOU DECIDE which notes to take

Okay, so then: what does "own the project" mean?

In screenwriting, if someone pays you to write -- **they own** what you wrote.

But! If someone says: *"gee, I **might** pay for it...if you changed it like **this**,"* or *"I know what other people pay for, and I say change **this**..."*

-- it's **your** script and you have to think about how much you want to do what they say.

Some things to think about as you decide:

Notes Are OPINIONS
When you're desperate to break in, you feel like you have to do what anyone "inside" says. But do remember legendary screenwriter William Goldman's immortal insight:

"NOBODY KNOWS ANYTHING"

Even the famous and powerful are just guessing. We are all desperate for an absolute-sure-thing right answer...but scripts are an art.

I personally think it's good to get a bunch of people to read your work. A good read is hard to find; getting more improves the odds. (Being really "strategic" about who you show your work to is for producers and agents. I think a writer should want everyone to read their work all the time.)

A variety of reads also helps you see: the same work will get impossibly different notes. They will be smart, well-reasoned and stated with conviction. They will also be...just opinions.

Consider The Agenda And Values Of The Note-Giver.
Almost everyone you can ask to read a script will be in -- or wanting to be in -- The Industry, so they are not reading like an audience. They are reading for what they need.

Do they "get" your project?

Are their notes consistent with the other choices in the script?

Are they giving you notes to change your project into something else? If it's a little indie film and they are telling you how it can become an epic TV series...you want to think before you take that note.

Look for people who embrace what your project is, and give notes about making that better.

What Is Your Goal In Asking For Notes?
Don't look for a summary judgment on your talent or future.

**notes can only be an opinion on
THE WORK
NOT on whether you are worthy**

Try to listen for -- or even ask about -- specific issues, especially things you feel uncertain about:

did the plot make sense to them?

did they care about the main character?

did the dialogue feel real?

did it move too slow, or too fast?

did they get the point, the message, the feeling?

This Is Going To Sting A Bit

Even though you asked for it, being analyzed and criticized produces a kind of stress. One may sign up to be a soldier, but it still hurts to get shot.

Part of being an artist is agreeing to be judged, all the time.

You can't write in such a way that everyone will like what you do. You can't "follow the rules" and check off every box and get a perfect score.

Make choices you can live with, even when someone doesn't like them.

Notes are Valuable

It would be so easy if they were always wrong!

You need them.

Some will instantly make sense to you, they will make you think: *"Yeah, when I wrote that, I knew it was off -- but it was the best I could do at the moment,"* or maybe, *"Holy crap, I didn't realize that but of course, it's true."*

Take those notes. Do something about them.

But even when this doesn't happen, even when they're **wrong** --

notes still might show you something you need to think about.

Especially if different people give a similar note -- even if they define it in different ways or think different things will solve it: that's a note you want to pay attention to.

What To Do When You Get Notes
Most of the time, a writer's job when getting notes is:

**writing them down
taking them in**

so that **later**...you can:

**TRANSLATE notes
into workable plans & questions**

You almost always need to translate notes. Most people who give notes aren't writers -- or they are writers who only think their own way. That's all okay.

It's **your** job to turn what they say into a useful form for **you.**

Sort Out The Problems From The Solutions
Even if you don't agree with their solution, the problem may be real.

Think about what the note is talking about, and approach it in your own way.

Translate Negative Responses Into Positive Actions
Despite (usually) good intentions -- many people simply tell you what's wrong with your work. That doesn't really help much.

Turn negative notes into something you can **do**.

Look For "The Note Behind The Note"

For example, someone will say the script is missing something -- even though you can show them: the words are **there**, right on the page.

But they didn't have an impact. So maybe:

there's too much else around it

it's not said clearly enough

it's in the wrong place

it's not played out in the story

It's always worth asking yourself, even if a note is truly wrong, what might be behind it.

Take A Breath

No matter what you feel -- excited or devastated -- take some time. Don't react or respond right away. Let yourself work through it.

And no matter what -- good, bad or indifferent, notes will be **A LOT**. So:

Pay Attention To How You Always React

Different work, different people, should make for different experiences. So if you keep having the same experience, over and over...think about why.

If you **always** feel: *"I have to do what they say,"* or *"Forget it, I can't work with this person,"* -- then it's about **you**, not the work or the note.

Try to start hearing the notes as being about that specific work, instead of whatever personal thing is being triggered by this experience.

This is where that "take a breath" thing comes in handy.

Learn To Notice When You're Feeling It's Personal

Does it feel like it's about you? You are being hurt or attacked? Your life, your future are being threatened?

It's not -- and you're not.

(Well, sometimes people are awful and **do** attack you...ideally you'll know the difference and take care of yourself.)

Stop and look at those feelings. Ask yourself what they mean to you, what they do for you. Think about what you expect, what this situation reminds you of.

"But I Like It That Way"

Even when you get good notes, you still may want to do it your own way. This is both cringe-y and the core of being an artist -- so it is really hard to know which one is going on at any given moment.

One key way to tell is: are you aware that what you want is a choice?

If you **want** it to be kinda boring, or too expensive for the genre, or to be your directorial debut...that's fine, but you have to be willing to pay the price for that choice.

Should You Defend Your Work?

You asked them to read because you wanted their opinion. Are you trying to convince them they're wrong? You probably won't.

My main advice on arguing a note: do it **once**. If it works: yay! If it doesn't: let it go.

If you **do** defend your work:

Beware Defending Your Choices With Rules
Don't try to justify your work with some grand authority or theory. If it's not working in your work, for this reader -- it doesn't matter how much you understand some rule.

Beware Defending Your Choices With Other work
Don't defend your script by saying, "it's like a scene in (some other movie.)" Not only is it not a valid defense (i.e. **this** apple must taste sweet, because **that** one did) -- it's also a red flag that you may be carrying the inspiration of another work into your judgement of your own.

It's only valid if someone says "that type of thing you did **can't** work" – and you need to show them it can.

Beware Defending Something Because It Took A Lot Of Work To Get It
In fact, difficult effort might even be a sign that it should go. Ask yourself...*am I just clinging to this because it was hard to do?*

Does The Note "Click"?
I know this is vague but it's a real thing: even if you're miserable about the amount of work it's going to take or the losses it will require, a note should make sense to you and **feel** like something got better.

Dealing With The "Alternate Universe Note"
You may get notes steering you to a **valid different** version of

your work.

There's nothing wrong with exploring a new version of your idea. If it feels like this new approach is really interesting or worthwhile...try it.

NEVER throw away your original work!
SAVE A COPY
you may want to go back to it

The last thing I want to say regarding notes: they are part of the process. One thing you learn as a professional is:

Screenwriting Means Endless Changes
A key skill for screenwriters is the ability to work up a detailed, coherent, fully-realized understanding of the story and characters -- and then toss it out and come up with another, just as good.

You can look at this as cause for despair, because how can we make choices or have any sense of good and bad if everything can change?

But if you just look it as a skill, like improvisation: *okay -- let's see what we can do with it this way.*

Then it's incredibly liberating and empowering.

4 THINGS TO KNOW

There is no "right way" to become an artist.

This is one of the hardest things to accept about art -- it seems like there are rules and systems but the truth is: **every artist has to make their own path.**

This doesn't mean that you can do anything you want. You work within your reality: who you are, what you love, what you do well, your circumstances and resources.

So you need to get information and try to understand your reality, in order to make your choices.

Know The Art

Be an artist who endlessly studies art and says:

> *look at all the different ways to do this thing!*
> *what can I learn from this one?*
> *how does it work?*
> *what can I use?*

There has never been a time like this for self-education. It does not have to cost a lot. Don't wait, don't look for some authority to tell you what to do.

Learn About The Rest Of The Filmmaking Process

If you want to work with filmmakers, get some sense of what they do, the problems they face, what happens to your script when it goes into production.

Read or watch interviews and how-to books or videos about

directing, acting, producing, cinematography, editing, etc.

Know Screen History
This helps you see the endless possibilities and keeps you from getting pushed around by theory.

Everything that everyone else has ever done is a tool for you to use. Those who do not remember the past are unable to steal from it.

Delve deeply into your chosen genre or style or tradition. But also look outside your comfort zone. There are entirely different languages using the same tools. You might not always have fun, but you can learn from it.

Read Scripts
(For more detail about reading-as-a-screenwriter, see the chapter "Take Art Apart.")

Get Behind The Scenes
When you study finished work, it all seems so inevitable. Explore behind-the-scenes reports to see the petty, wrongheaded, compromised or bizarre motives behind seemingly inevitable choices.

Look at memoirs, biographies, interviews, documentaries, books and podcasts; commentary tracks; magazines, videos of panel discussions from film festivals and conferences.

Great art has a magic, magnetic power. Demystify it.

Know Other Arts
Novels show you how to make a sentence flow and shape a paragraph. Theater teaches you to create character and story through dramatic action and dialogue.

Screen narrative is made up of so many other arts. Get a feel for photography, painting, poetry, comics and graphic arts, video games, music.

Know The Business

Read or watch interviews with producers, agents, managers, readers, executives.

Many artists talk about their experiences in the business. Substacks, blogs, podcasts, film festival and screenwriting conference interviews and panel discussions.

Check out sources of entertainment business news like *The Hollywood Reporter, Deadline, Variety, Indiewire*: hires, fires, deals, what's going into production.

If you can (it's not easy) try to talk with people working in the business -- to learn, not to "network." While big names at the top of the pyramid are exciting, you may learn more from those doing the everyday work, the assistants, employees and crew.

Know The World

Life is an endless idea factory, full of amazing stories. Every writer is to some extent a voyeur, a reporter, a detective, a psychologist, a historian and a thief.

The more you learn about how other people live and think and feel, the better you'll write. What parts of experience are shared? What is unique to a place, time, society, occupation? How do you capture those things, convey them?

Read nonfiction: history, psychology, philosophy, biography, sociology. The news. True crime. Memoirs.

There has never been a time like this for getting into other people's lives. Videos, essays, podcasts, journals, online communities, documentaries, blogs and Substacks.

Get out among people, especially people who are different from you.

Keep your eyes open. Study the world: look at it, taste it. Think about the stories of people you meet, the ones you see. Delve into the pain and the joy of it all.

Know Yourself

You can be a fan of all sorts of amazing things, the business can want what it wants, you can train yourself to be better at skills or write in the formula of the moment...but in the end: you really can only do what you do, the best you can.

Know Your Process
are you the sort of person who works in short bursts, or long sessions?

do you work best in quiet or a bit of chaos?

what are you good at, creatively?

what are you good at professionally/business-wise?

what do you need to get better at?

how do you handle criticism?

how good are you at self-analysis?

how resilient are you?

how flexible, self-motivated, organized?

Think About What You Want

what do you care about?

what is worth doing even if it fails?

what are you willing to do?

what are you willing give up?

what are your resources?

Why are you writing? Be honest. Think about what you're trying to get out of it.

praise?

status?

money?

access to people you admire?

the pleasure of making things?

exploring or resolving something in your life?

the desire to make a statement?

the playing-out of fears and fantasies, living alternate lives?

Think realistically about how you could find a path to do these things. Think in small steps.

Look at what you do instinctively, your strengths and weaknesses. Try to see how you're wired, and what you can change. Make work plans that fit who you are.

The things you like may not be the things you do best. It's usually helpful to accept your reality and create within it.

Try to do what you love, even if you can't do it the way you imagine. That's all any of us can do.

figure out what you do well, and what you don't

figure out how to survive, doing what you do

**try to plan a path that will make the most of what
you do**

know the art
know the business
know the world
know yourself

This is not instead of writing, nor before writing. Writing comes first. Nothing else matters if you're not doing the work. This is stuff to do in your (ha-ha-ha) spare time.

CONTEST VS. LIBRARY

I believe there are two ways to look at art: as a contest, or as a library.

Are both equally valid? No. One doesn't really work.

Unfortunately -- it's the one that most people use.

art is NOT a contest

It's just not. For example: in a race (a form of contest), all the runners are **doing the same thing** -- but in "art contests" (like ratings or box office) you're pitting different genres and styles against each other, even though they have different goals, audiences and values.

Even within a genre or style: the whole point of art is to create a **unique** work -- and therefore **not doing the same thing.**

"Art contests" are mostly popularity or sales contests: how many people clicked or viewed or bought tickets. In theory, this shows what the audience wants -- except some contestants are in more theaters, were pushed by an algorithm, or have more advertising.

So in art contests we've essentially got contestants playing different sports on different types of field.

Why are we still taking this seriously?

Regarding awards: some voters have specialized knowledge, so if you want to know what sound mixers think is the "best sound mixing"...sure: take that seriously.

Except:

What does "best art" even mean?

The fastest runner is the best runner because **speed** is what is being measured in a race.

But what is being **measured** when we talk about "best art"?

Whether one work is funnier or scarier or more emotional than another is a matter of opinion. And whether being funny or scary or emotional is even a **good thing** is also a matter of opinion.

Do you know of any work of art about which people **don't** have conflicting opinions? Even within one person -- our opinions of what's good can be different at different times of our lives.

So art **cannot be** a contest, because there is no meaningful way to **measure winning.**

If you value melody and harmony, then a punk band is incompetent. If you value a painting that looks like something in real life, then abstract art is not even art.

In art, a person running the opposite way isn't necessarily losing the race -- they may just be playing a different game.

But it gets even worse: the set of values for the companies running our art contests is: *what will make us money?* So if an artist or audience isn't likely to be profitable enough...they don't even get to play.

And that's how you know a library is right and a contest is wrong:

a library lets you have a contest
but a contest doesn't let you have
a library

In a library, you don't throw out the runner going the wrong way, you put them on the shelf for running in that direction. Maybe it's way in a back room and you have to really hunt to find it -- but it's there.

You put minor work in a library, and influential-but-no longer-powerful work, and work that's not good but is interesting for other reasons.

They're important to keep because, when judging art, you don't just ask who got what number, you analyze and compare the works to understand the difference. It's not just: this is better and this is worse -- it's: what's good about this and what's not and **why**. Or even: this isn't good but I can learn from it.

But then, does a "library" mean you put **everything** in? Even work by an amateur, an outsider, a hopeless incompetent?

Remember: I'm talking about a **frame of mind**, here -- a way of looking at art and artists -- and in **those** terms: yes.

If we throw stuff out of the game because it doesn't sell or isn't popular -- then lots of good art "failed" the contests of their time: Vincent Van Gogh, Emily Dickinson, *It's A Wonderful Life* and *Moby Dick*.

But forget about "the neglected great." That misses the real point:

If you love an art, you don't just want the winners, the greatest hits, the top 40. You want the whole deep dive, the weird variations, the influences, the failed experiments, even the disasters.

I am not saying we should get rid of ratings, rankings, critics and awards.

Contests have value. They recognize and reward quality and accomplishment. They drive people to aspire and achieve:

wanting to be seen as the best, or to have the biggest hit, is the legit and serious engine behind a lot of great art.

Plus there is too much stuff. We **do** need some way to sort out all this "content," and a contest narrows it down.

I'm just saying: if you're an artist, think about why you want to "win" at art.

If you want to win because you're trying to get the support to do more work -- great: play the game. We live in the real world, art is a business and being ranked **can** get you more money and more freedom to do what you want. But recognize that the contest is not measuring what it says and taking the contest too seriously may be harmful to doing your best work.

Figure out what being in the game is worth to you, and maybe figure out ways to get rewards and be seen beyond the contest.

Art isn't about winning. It's about capturing this world and this life in all its complicated variety, stirring up feelings and making us think and taking our minds off our troubles.

If you're doing that...if you're **trying** to do that: you can't lose.

RETHINK SUCCESS

It is very hard to understand work from the outside.

Especially work with a "public face" -- like politics: we hear about the most exalted positions, the big winners (or notorious losers). We don't hear much about the community council, the deputy assistant, the mid-level department...but those are what we would likely be doing, if we worked in that field.

My favorite example is the Olympics:

In 2024, there were 10,500 Olympians competing in Paris, and only 1,044 medals were given out. So about 90% of Olympic athletes -- the best-of-the-best in their field -- were "losers." They were not the story.

And of that top 10%, only maybe a dozen or so got serious media attention. So we really only know about .01%.

If we wanted to be an Olympic athlete: what would we know about the reality of doing this work? About what it's like to be in the game but not the winner?

Screenwriting is also a job with a "public face." The Writer's Guild Of America (the screenwriters union in the USA) has about 12,000 members. It is very competitive to get in. But most members -- the "Olympians of screenwriting" -- are on writing staffs or doing drafts of features that other writers will also work on.

In other words: you have never heard of them.

**you need to get past the
public mythology of success
if you actually want to do the work**

You have a story in your mind about your career.

Think about what that is and where you got it from -- and what you're going to do if it doesn't turn out to be your story.

Because if you get too fixed on one story -- the public face -- you make your choices with blinders on, and might walk right past an open door to accomplishment and joy.

Most people outside of the arts define a "real" artist as "professional" -- meaning you make money from the work.

But what if you sell your art at a street fair -- making money, but not enough to live on? What if you work in an art form -- local theater, folk crafts, painting, opera, poetry --- that just doesn't usually make money?

Are you a "real" artist?

The screenwriting success story goes like this: you write an original script, someone buys it and makes it, and then you decide what you want to do next.

That **almost never** happens. It's a freak occurrence.

Would you feel like a success if this was your story:

You write a movie that gets made, but other writers work on it, too -- so you end up with no credit. You got paid, you're a professional screenwriter but no one knows.

A wealthy person pays you a weekly salary for the year it takes to write a vanity project that only they will read.

You're hired to write a script for a studio and they like it -- but the head of the studio gets fired, so your script is put on a shelf forever.

You write an episode of television, and get the money and credit -- but by the time it goes through rewrites there isn't a single line you wrote left in it.

You write something you love, and people in The Industry love it too -- but it's offbeat and nobody can get it made.

You make a little DIY indie movie that's artistically satisfying to you and critically acclaimed, speaks on an under-explored topic to a neglected audience who feel it's powerful...but it's unimportant to The Industry and you have to pay for it yourself.

(All of these things happened to me.)

I'm not here to tell you what success is. I just want you to ask:

what is success, to me?

The real story is that there are different **kinds** of success in art -- and you get different things from them:

money
acclaim
popularity
opportunity
personal growth
using your voice
creative control

Often you have to sacrifice some for the one you want most. For example, you can have creative control but you have to give up money. You can have steady work on a writing staff, but less acclaim.

That's why you need to be open to whatever story your career turns out to be.

Work toward these things:

the pleasure of figuring out a story

making a character come alive or coming up with a line

writing something **you think** is good

making a statement work that gives you comfort -- or a kick

making progress getting better

the awe you feel at simply having made something

the joy of finding and using your own voice and vision

Now and then, people -- a lot or a few -- will say: *that was good.* Someone will get wrapped up in the imaginary place and time you made, will laugh or cry or understand. That is success.

you have NO CONTROL over the fate of your work

nothing you can do in a work of art
will ensure a particular outcome

you do this kind of work to see
how it comes out

You create to connect. You can't control if you connect with one person or a handful or a million.

In many ways: one matters more.

HOW TO SUCCEED

The single consistent element in all stories of artistic success is chance.

Every hit, every legend, at some crucial point -- perhaps because of who they met or how society or business was structured -- got lucky

So much creative advice is based in "analyzing success." But in art, explanations of why something becomes a hit verge on nonsense. (Look at all the other work that did the same thing and failed.)

It is important to be talented and work hard, but that is not enough. You can do everything right, but still never be paid or recognized. You can be an idiot and have a celebrated hit.

As far as I can tell, this is the best path to make success possible:

step 1: make yourself ready for luck
develop your skills and process
do good work
over and over again

step 2: make yourself available to luck
show your work
put it out there somehow
over and over again

step 3: make a life that will support steps 1 & 2
build a sustainable, healthy, comfortable life
in which to work
even if you do not get lucky

...and then keep taking these three steps, over and over again.

THE BUSINESS

I am not great with the business stuff.

I am surprised I managed to survive it as long as I did. I didn't really understand the job during most of the time I did it. Plus I am stubborn, self-centered and difficult.

There is plenty of advice out there about the business. I urge you to seek out current information from a variety of sources.

That said, what follows are a few thoughts on the business.

CAREER ADVICE IN A TIME OF CHAOS

The most important thing you need to know:

EVERYTHING is changing
MORE THAN EVER BEFORE

We are in the midst of **the most substantial changes** in the history of the screen business.

In the first phase of film history, at the beginning of the 20th century, there were countless little companies, very disorganized and volatile. But in the 1920s, the major studios consolidated and the "factory system" took over. For the next fifty years a handful of studios monopolized The Industry. They owned the theater chains, so it was impossible for anyone else to distribute movies.

These monopolies were shaken by anti-trust decisions and television during the 1950s and 1960s, but in the 1970s all of the major studios were taken over by larger corporations -- essentially re-monopolizing them. The same system and the same players still ran The Industry, with a new corporate mandate to keep doing what they had been doing, but bigger -- especially regarding merchandising and international markets.

So, this is a fairly-accurate portrait of the entire history of the American screen business:

Until...

In the 2000s, new companies -- notably Netflix, Amazon and Apple -- came in with a **whole new distribution system**: digital distribution, which we mostly call "streaming."

This is **really important.** **I cannot** emphasize this enough:

DISTRIBUTION is the engine
of the entertainment business

The studios, networks and streaming services are **distribution companies.** You may think they are in the business of making movies and shows -- but they only make stuff so they have a reliable source of things to distribute.

Previous new distribution technologies (television, videotape, DVD) rattled the system -- but were quickly absorbed into it (they were called "windows": steps that a studio project passed through.)

The tech companies didn't compete within this system -- they built an alternative, which took an ever-increasing portion of the audience with astonishing speed.

The larger studios and networks quickly and frantically gave up their own system and have tried to join or imitate the new distribution model.

Everything in The Industry has been in turmoil ever since.

Among the changes -- all happening very fast:

A New System
The tech companies have radically different business methods, sources of income, metrics of success.

Sales of tickets or physical media, the previous methods of taking in money, are no longer important. The Industry now runs on subscriptions, watch time, library development, online attention and sale of devices. Algorithms, social media and direct measurement of audience response now steer what we see and what gets made.

No Single Unified Audience
In theory, everybody can watch what they want, when they want it. (In reality, a few companies completely control what we have access to.)

This allows new audiences to be taken seriously and new voices to speak. But it also means the audience has been broken into niches, silos, and echo-chambers.

At the same time, the tech companies and their distribution system are global. (While the old American studios certainly made sure to export their wares around the world, it was very much a one-way traffic.)

Changing the audience in two conflicting directions -- toward niches, but also global scale -- has complicated the culture of screen storytelling.

Art tends to thrive within limits. Having to be all things to a lot of very different people in very different cultures makes it very hard to be as distinctive, unique and specific as good art has to be.

New Forms Of Art Are Developing

Digital technology also has brought us whole new art forms, which are cutting into the screen-story audience, and competing for the prized place in the cultural center.

The series seems to have taken over from the movie as our main storytelling format, while videogames, podcasts, short-form and user-generated-video and social media are pulling the audience in new directions.

Digital technology has changed society as a whole. The Digital Revolution is having an equivalent impact to The Renaissance or The Industrial Revolution...but those took place over centuries, this is happening within a single generation.

Art and entertainment come from within a society and culture... and currently ours are in flux. Radical changes are taking place in our government, education, business, communications, relationships and even possibly the structure of our brains.

WE ARE NOT DONE

We are still in the early stages of all this. Everyone is still figuring it out as we go along. We really can't predict the meaning and impact of most of these changes.

We can watch a screen narrative on a phone, tablet, computer, 70-inch TV, game console, IMAX theater, VR headset, the back of an airline seat, a website or channel.

We're like Wiley Coyote after he's run off the cliff and is still running in mid-air when he realizes: *things have changed under my feet.*

I am not an expert on the digital revolution. I advise you to study it, track it, explore it.

But I personally believe these things will be true in the near future:

Everything Is Streaming

Broadcast may hang around, but most people will consume most art and entertainment digitally.

Most screenwriting work will be on the staffs of series.

The "movie" form will live on. People will still want to watch self-contained stories in one sitting -- but they'll watch 'em on streaming.

Theatrical movies will be what Broadway is to theater: big events only. Small independent movie houses will flourish locally.

Consolidated Distribution -- But A Rich Outsider Landscape

As in theater, music, publishing and tech: power and money in screen entertainment will increasingly be consolidated into a few large companies.

But online you'll find more small, local or niche communities available to artists.

Unions vs Gigs

I suspect this consolidation will mean increasing attempts to get rid of unions. If you truly believe we're better without unions, just check who's getting rich and who's not.

More Opportunity To Be An Artist -- But For Less Money

Inequality will rise. While the few big consolidated distributors will rake in a lot of money and therefore pay a few hit-makers well, most artists will be playing small venues, passing the hat, working day jobs.

Digital production and distribution has made it possible for anyone, anywhere to "put on a show in our old barn"...and present it to the world.

The problem is: getting anyone to watch it, because there is so much stuff coming at us all every day.

So:
EVERYTHING is changing
MORE THAN EVER BEFORE

And my advice is:
you might as well be you

Currently each company has its own formula for what they want to buy or make -- which they keep secret, and change very frequently.

This opacity and churn are new. The companies are changing their plans faster than the time it takes to write or produce a project. This means artists can't choose what to create based on what's being bought. By the time it is written or made, the trend will have shifted.

So your best chance to get "picked" is simply to be distinctly what you are -- and hope that someone with money and power happens to want that.

get good at what you do
the people who hire writers want to know you
have the skills to work on demand, understand notes,
take whatever assignment is thrown at you
and deliver on time

produce new work and show it around
don't wait for permission or approval
develop your SKILLS by doing the work
show us your VISION by doing the work

DIY is more available than ever, small scale local work is more possible than ever -- and those things are more important than ever.

Work within your means. Make a sustainable work life, wherever you are, at whatever scale you can.

Strip down to simple and self-sufficient. Don't try to beat the big companies at their game. Know yourself. Explore all the technology. Be open to new forms of art.

do what you can
as who you are
with what you have
right now

Choose your path, which really means choose your **next few steps.** Have a general direction you're headed in but do not try to plan your whole career.

You're on a river. It's moving; you move **within** that motion. Learn to read the surface, to see the signs there are rocks and currents underneath. Look at whats happening to the other rafts.

Even in the most stable times, no one is in control of their creative career. In times of chaos, try to survive and look for opportunities.

do what you do
do it a lot
do it well

If you never get lucky, if they never open up that checkbook or put you out on their screens, at least you did what you love.

Which is a rare thing in life, and even more so in The Industry.

everything is chaos

you might as well be you

WHAT WORKING SCREENWRITERS REALLY DO

For most professionals, the job is to be a skilled worker, to bring your talents and abilities to a project that someone else owns and controls.

Currently (spring 2025) most working screenwriters in the US are on the writing staff of a series. Some are hired to rewrite other people's scripts or to adapt a property (like a book, videogame, or toy) owned by a company.

A lot of people in the business use writers as a tool for their thinking process. You try stuff out, so they can decide what they think. This is obviously easier on them, and harder on you.

Everyone you work for has an agenda, and your job is to help them create documents that serve their agenda.

The job is to:

> be flexible deliver on time, as agreeably as possible
> understand how the work is done in The Industry
> create a text, not explanations or promises
> mostly rewriting, and being rewritten
> bring your best, but understand where the power is, and admit you are powerless.

A lot of a professional writer's time is spent trying to get work. You must come up with detailed pitches for projects, and often rewrite or rethink them several times, as a part of the "audition" process. This can take weeks or months.

You are going to lose your job. Most don't last very long. Plus screenwriters get fired a lot. Most companies like the idea of having writers rewrite each other. The Industry wants to go shopping, and you are an item in the supermarket aisle.

I believe one way to explain the screenwriter's job:

**find your version of
the center, the heart, of the work --
in the form of a story and characters**

put it on the page in script form

fight for it

lose gracefully

try again

HOW TO GET AN AGENT

Agents are important to writers. It's almost impossible to get companies to read your work, or to get a job in The Industry, without one.

Agents show your work to The Industry and recommend you for jobs. They negotiate your deals and contracts. They collect your pay, take out commissions for themselves and managers and lawyers, and give the rest to you. They also may give you career guidance, read your work and give notes. Some even become your friends and let you sleep on their sofa when you're just starting out and you visit LA (thank you, Lisa Callamaro!)

But there is very little you can do right now to get an agent.

Agents Show Up When There Is Money Involved

They do not have time for you, unless you and your work are something they can sell right this moment. This is even true when you are their client.

When you have a job offer, someone wanting to buy your script, or maybe win a big contest -- then agents will talk to you.

On the bright side:

An Agent Is Not Going To Magically Make Everything Better

Most writers feel their agents don't do much for them.

Agents are overloaded. Some have a **lot** of clients. That's a lot of contracts to read, scripts to read, phone calls to make. They have a difficult job. It is hard to sell scripts. There are too many. Things sell -- or don't -- for bizarre reasons.

Most are employees of agencies, where they are judged by how much money they bring in and how many powerful clients they have. It's very high-pressure, very zero-sum. They can't even just take on a client. They have to sell you to the agency, which means a bunch of really stressed aggressive salespeople are judging how much money they think you can make them.

Your agent may care about you, but they still have to prove their worth to the company by bringing in more and more money or they get fired.

Therefore, a client or project that will bring in more money is going to be put first. And if a script is difficult to sell or not going to be very big, why would they prioritize it?

Also, agents are people. Some are kind, smart and supportive... while some are not.

Here's what to do when you don't have an agent:

get better at what you do

do everything else
look for producers, directors, actors --
even if they are just starting out too --
work with them, get stuff made

have a new, great script
agents do not want to see old work
have a bunch scripts in the works

THE "LOG LINE"

A script must be "sold" over and over again. Each person who likes it will have to bring it to collaborators, agents, producers, executives, production companies, financiers, networks, studios or distributors. And they all have too much to read.

So they want a one-or-two sentence description: a "log line."

(So named because companies keep a log of every script they receive, and historically that log only had space for a very short summary.)

A log line tries to convey:

> the genre
> the central character and their world
> their problem or goal
> the twist or unexpected element that makes this unique

It ought to assure a reader that *"I know what this is…"* and yet also make them think: *"How is **that** gonna work?"*

The **only** purpose of a log line is to hook, to lure, to provoke a reader to think: ***I WANT TO READ THIS.***

So don't give away the ending.

The long line will not capture the complexity and depth of your work.

The value of this crude, reductive tool for a writer: it helps you think out what you're offering the audience. If you can't find a log line for your script, you may not have a grasp on your project yet, or it may be dangerously (or artistically-but-not-commercially) disorganized.

This does not mean your **work** has to be shallow and formulaic. Even the most complex works of literature can be viewed, honestly, through this lens: *"A dark action adventure story about an innocent young sailor who signs on to a whaling ship commanded by a madman hell-bent on confronting a monstrous whale."*

The log line is a necessary tool for navigating The Industry, but it is also a useful way to step back and get perspective while working. Think of the simplification as a way of trying to name the narrative heart.

ARTIFICIAL INTELLIGENCE

Let's pretend it works. Let's be generous and pretend that AI actually can create art, in the mysterious human sense of that phrase.

Why would you ask it to do that for you? Would you ask (or pay) another human being to write part of your work?

A lot of writers have told me they would use AI to write their rough draft or to brainstorm ideas.

Do you think the choices made in those steps of the writing process don't matter? That they don't reflect the mind or spirit of the artist? That there is some generic portion of writing you don't have to be creative for?

Seriously?

You certainly would be able to write faster with AI. Faster, in fact, than you can actually write...which would be no different from getting in a car and driving part of a marathon. I'm not talking about credit -- I'm saying that you would have made the phrase "I ran that race" (or "I wrote that story") meaningless.

My objection is not technological. I love my technological tools. But there is a fatal difference between being able to cut-and-paste and having my computer choose what to cut or where to paste it.

Even if we accept the highly-debatable notion that human brains are simply "biological computers" processing earlier "inputs" and spitting out the resulting art: the values according to which a human artist "processes" are unique to that person.

So when you use AI you are essentially asking it to think for you.

But let's stop pretending. It is important to recognize that AI is not actually "writing." It's averaging, predicting according to a set of programmed values which you do not control. And AI's values are often simply the most popular response -- or worse, the response steered by a company toward its values, needs or sponsors.

Making art is making choices.

Even if that means you're slow in making them, or make them badly.

Don't let your tools make your choices.

STRAY BITS

Since feelings and inspirations come to us magically, it seems like art should, too.

But art is work. You have to learn the skills that go into it, and work at them, over time.

===

Seek out experience.

No matter how much talent you have, how much you have studied or practiced: until you have gone through production, distribution and exhibition -- until you've put work out to an audience -- you don't even know what you don't know.

It can be school, local theater, online videos or the artistic equivalent of a sidewalk lemonade stand.

It can be a crappy experience, that's fine. It's still an experience, and you will learn from it as from nothing else.

===

Create a sustainable life.

Prepare for years of unpaid work.

Assume it won't pay off.

Don't borrow. Don't gamble more than you can afford to lose.

Find a way to pay your bills.

Build a writing process that can work while you work.

===

The impact of art is deep and serious, but when you work in the arts you have to face the fact that everybody kind of over-sells it.

In the end, even the **greatest** work of art...it's just a picture or a book or a movie or a show.

How many times have you finished watching something great, even life-changing...and then after a while you said: *okay, what else can I watch?*

===

Remember that what producers and executives do is brutally hard.

They are trying to sell a thing that doesn't exist, in a fiercely competitive power game within an irrational business. They have massive piles of mostly inept crap to read, horrible pitching sessions to sit through. They have to make decisions that require trusting talent. Writers usually let them down.

All during this they have to pretend they are cool, powerful and know what they are doing.

===

All work Above The Line (i.e, between writers, actors, directors and producers) is a series of negotiations between different versions of the movie.

===

Don't trust anyone who won't give you facts or details.

Watch out for people who over-promise, see if they follow through.

Try not to work with anyone who lies to you. This will be more difficult than you'd think.

===

A good producer is what gets most projects made.

Agents churn through flavor-of-the-minute market values. Producers attach themselves to projects and work on them for years.

You're most likely to find an aspiring or beginning producer. You can rise together. They may not be able to pay, but they'll invest their effort.

It is legit for a producer to ask to be "attached" to a project with a letter, or to ask for an option. It is **not** legit for a producer to ask you for money.

===

Get a lawyer involved in options/attachments/deals or any contracts with anyone. An entertainment lawyer is nice but any lawyer is better than none.

It's a drag, but it's a good idea.

===

The work of selling and the work of writing are different.

Your job is writing.

Take advice on selling after you do your job.

===

There is no "career endgame." Artistic careers are not organized around an end. You never hear artists saying, "I can't wait until I can stop doing this and retire."

===

One of the hardest things about becoming an artist is learning how to make your own choices, to find and follow your instincts. But as a screenwriter, after you do that -- others decide what's right and wrong, and tell you to follow their instincts. Being able to live with that is the heart of being a professional.

===

No matter how good you get, opinions are hell for artists.

Think about your favorite movies, shows, books, music -- now think about everyone's opinions on it.

Yeah: it's hell.

===

Becoming a professional writer takes time and many scripts.

 Give yourself a break, and be real about the work this takes.

Prepare for the 10,000 hours.

===

Hope for the best but prepare for the worst.

===

Nothing is real until it is in the past tense.

Anything can change, for unforeseen reasons. Nothing will come out as planned. Movies fall apart. Companies fold. People get fired.

Almost no one you work with has the power to make something happen, no matter how much they want it.

===

Almost everyone in the business likes to piss on stuff, to mark it, to make it their own.

But, to be fair, this is also a part of creativity.

===

The purpose of creative preparation is to make you ready for the inevitable moment when the thing can't be done as planned.

===

Most people in The Industry will be lying to themselves more than actually trying to deceive you – but the end result is the same.

===

A few artists get a "big break," but most have a series of little breaks.

If you spend all your time looking for the big break, you may not make the most of, or enjoy, the little ones.

Be whatever size you are and be good at it.

===

Every big hit film could easily be (and often was) turned down because of the very elements that made it work.

The only thing that makes a film a happen is the enthusiasm of a powerful person.

None of this is within your control, none of it can be predicted.

The one thing that makes it more likely is to work at the absolute top of your talent.

===

The Industry assumes everything is negotiable.

Everyone is willing to do whatever it takes to please the powerful.

===

The great thing about writing is: no one can stop you from doing it.

===

People in The Industry often don't want to hear about the consequences of changes they ask for.

===

Never assume that one day there will be a project you don't have to fight for. The greatest, most celebrated and powerful filmmakers still have to fight.

===

It is always good to write a new script.

Why would you **not**?

Keep writing new scripts until you have nothing left to learn or say.

===

Get something real in your work. Give us something -- even if it is small -- from your experience or feelings. Something you care about, that you believe is true or important.

===

Having a work method helps you write under difficult circumstances.

This is useful because circumstances are almost always somewhat difficult.

===

You know what stops people from writing? Wondering if it's good enough. It's gonna be as good as it's gonna be, and you can't know until you do it.

===

Don't go looking to other scripts or trends or even real life for answers to script problems.

Look at your script.

If you don't have a script: write a draft, because that's where the answer will be.

===

Writing should be fun.

You can't do something this personal, self-disciplined and solitary if it makes you miserable. Even when it is frustrating or difficult, you should feel good to at least be trying.

Look for what makes it fun, take that seriously. Work on that.

===

There are many ways to tell a story.

===

If you take the steps, the path will appear.

GO WRITE
SOMETHING

ACKNOWLEDGEMENTS

Let's start with everyone I have ever worked with, worked for, met with or been inspired by. Thank you. And I apologize. But among that sea of names, some especially managed (or tried) to steer, support, advise or defuse me:

My agent and friend for decades, Lisa Callamaro. My managers Charlie Gogolak and Rosalie Swedlin.

Mentors (alphabetically) Robert Benton, Greg Hoblit, Callie Khouri and Richard Price.

Producers (alphabetically) Mark Amin, Tyler Boehm, Jay Cohen, Karen Dare, Gregg Gilreath, Adam Hendricks, David Higgins, David Koplan, John H. Lang, Meg Lefauve, John Moser, Couper Samuelson, Lisa Tornell, Cami Winikoff, May Wuthrich.

Writers, readers and inspirations (alphabetically) Robert Bella, Bill Harper, and Russ Woody.

Lisanne Sartor, Colette Sartor and everyone at Cinestory.

Jill Chamberlain and Patricia Verducci for support and encouragement of my teaching.

Howard Michael Gould, who gave me astonishing opportunities and always helps me to hollow out when things are going great.

Peter Biegen, my inspiring arguer-in-chief.

Sy, Joan and Melissa.

Harry, for showing me YouTube -- and so much else.

And Jenn: you're the one.